MARTHA'S *FLOWERS*

MARTHA'S *FLOWERS*

A PRACTICAL GUIDE TO GROWING, GATHERING, AND ENJOYING

MARTHA STEWART WITH KEVIN SHARKEY

CLARKSON POTTER/PUBLISHERS NEW YORK

Copyright © 2018 by
Martha Stewart Living
Omnimedia, Inc.

All rights reserved.
Published in the United
States by Clarkson Potter/
Publishers, an imprint
of the Crown Publishing
Group, a division of
Penguin Random House
LLC, New York.
clarksonpotter.com
marthastewart.com

CLARKSON POTTER is a
trademark and POTTER
with colophon is a
registered trademark
of Penguin Random
House LLC.

Library of Congress
Cataloging-in-
Publication Data
is available.

ISBN 978-0-307-95477-0
Ebook ISBN
978-0-307-95478-7

Printed in China

Design by Mary Jane
Callister
Cover photograph by
José Picayo; back cover
by Gabriela Herman.
Photograph credits
appear on page 283.

10 9 8 7 6 5 4 3 2 1

First Edition

*TO JUDE AND TRUMAN,
MY GRANDCHILDREN, FOR WHOM
I HAVE PLANTED MY GARDENS,
WITH HOPES OF INSTILLING IN THEM
THE SAME LOVE OF FLOWERS
THAT WAS ENGENDERED IN ME BY
MY FATHER MANY YEARS AGO.*

CONTENTS

INTRODUCTION

AS I WRITE THIS, I AM IN THE PROCESS OF planning my next garden. It will be my seventh garden, and I've been collecting images in my head, tear sheets in folders, and names of varieties of trees, shrubs, plants, and flowers that I think will be appropriate in this new and exciting landscape. And I've tried to imagine if this time will be any different from when I designed and dug (and double dug), then planted my very first, and very modest, garden in front of our tiny, white clapboard single-story cottage in the Berkshire mountains of Massachusetts.

It was my very own garden, where I was free from my father's beautifully modulated instructor's voice telling me what to do, and how to do it, in his backyard garden. Here, I was relaxed and confident that I could plant a noteworthy, productive garden.

At that time, my guidance came from my father, of course, but also from some wonderful books and places that influenced me profoundly: the writings of Vita Sackville-West, Gertrude Jekyll, and Helena Rutherfurd Ely, and the historic gardens that I loved visiting, including Monticello, Mount Vernon, the Mission House in nearby Stockbridge, and Old Sturbridge Village. Using a simple geometric plan, I laid out a front-path garden, which captured the sunlight for most of the day. Recycled bricks, carefully cleaned of all old rubble and cement, were laid in walks of stone dust and edged in more bricks laid on the diagonal. I discovered early on the beauty and efficacy of perennial planting, and most of the flowers there, in that small, pretty garden, were indeed perennials, interspersed with some herbs and very few annuals.

My most vivid memories of that garden were the hours spent tending the beds, singing to my young child, Alexis, making up fairy-tale-like stories about the flowers, reiterating the common as well as Latin names so that they are still ingrained not only in my head but also in hers. I was so proud when she could recite the flower names to my friends, pointing out her favorite campanula, digitalis, or *Papaver orientalis.*

The second, and the one that has been so instrumental in my subsequent development as a serious gardener, was the two-acre garden I designed and planted in Westport, Connecticut, on a perfect plot of south-facing land, and known as Turkey Hill. What began as two acres grew to four, and then in an orderly fashion to six as neighboring properties became available for purchase. Surrounding at first the 1805 farmhouse, which also played an important part in my entrepreneurial development, these gardens were my true testing ground, my "college education" for growing and experimenting, and my inspiration for putting pen to paper and writing books about

I am standing in my Summer House garden at Cantitoe Farm, a boxwood-enclosed area featuring a grove of several types of *Cotinus* (smoke bush), hostas, ferns, *Albizia julibrissin* (chocolate mimosa or silk tree), tree peonies, and lilies.

subjects I loved. My first gardening book, *Martha Stewart's Gardening: Month by Month*, appeared in 1991. In that book, I described the challenges and rewards of planting and growing not only flowers but also trees and vegetables and shrubs. In the beginning, I did most of the gardening myself, choosing the plant material, planning the layouts of the beds, placing the young trees in appropriate places, and weeding, fertilizing, watering, and grooming. I found that a half acre was doable, an acre not, and I hired my first two gardeners. They were not trained horticulturists, but they were very hardworking and each had a wonderful affinity for plants and their care. As my vision for the place expanded, they scurried to keep up, sometimes enlisting a brother or cousin to help. During this time, I traveled quite frequently to Europe and Asia, where I visited as many gardens as I could. My husband was a publisher, and he was working on *Visions of Paradise,* an extraordinary volume about Europe's most beautiful gardens. We traveled to England, France, and Italy to see with our own eyes the gardens so faithfully displayed in the photographs. It was on this trip that I started to understand the true nature of a real gardener, and the true worth of great garden and landscape design. I discovered the most famous landscape architects—in England, the Humphry Reptons, the William Kents, the Capability Browns; and in France, the René de Girardins, the André Le Nôtres, and the André Mollets. I bought books devoted to their works, and read with great interest why this and not that! I was even very influenced by Claude Monet after several visits to Giverny, and my flower garden emulated those gardens in intensity of color and types of flowers.

At Turkey Hill I made plenty of mistakes, but none that could not be remedied. I learned that gardening was enjoyment and sacrifice, that planting required inordinate patience and fortitude, and that instant gratification provided by planting large trees and established plants could be tempered with patience and smaller specimens, ultimately with better results.

While at Turkey Hill I purchased my third garden, Lily Pond, a one-acre parcel of land surrounding a large shingle-style nineteenth-century home on a beautiful tree-lined avenue in the village of East Hampton, Long Island. The climate, tempered by the proximity to the sea and the milder winters, was excellent for the cultivation of roses, and I was determined to grow a large assortment of old-world varieties—shrubs as well as climbers. I began a yearlong search for as many roses as I could find. Fortunately, there existed several excellent growers in the United States and Canada, and

I bought about six hundred bushes, the bare roots of which were delivered by post. For twenty-five years those bushes grew to produce very strong and beautiful blooms. The gardens perfumed the surrounding areas during June and July, and I was thrilled with the results. I studied the care and maintenance of roses, consulted great rosarians, and devised my own methods for successfully growing these amazing plants. We often featured those gardens in the pages of *Martha Stewart Living*. When the roses finally reached maturity, and began to decline from robust shrubs, I dug them all up and moved them to my farm in Katonah, a hamlet of Bedford, New York, hoping that a drastic change in climate and soil conditions might revive them. Happily, I can now report that they are thriving.

For a brief moment in time, I owned about forty-five acres in Greenfield Hill, Fairfield, Connecticut. I truly believed that there I could create my "big" garden, but I quickly realized that the soil, the location, and even the size of the property were not ideal for my biggest effort. I do count Greenfield Hill as one of my gardens, my fourth, but only because I planted some incredible trees there, and actually spent time developing a master plan for the landscape, which was never to be. And I do miss those trees—the gum tree with the flanged bark, the large-leafed *Magnolia grandiflora* trees, and the grove of mature gingko trees purchased from the New York Botanical Garden.

While looking for that special place, where I could live and commute from, I bought on a whim my "fifth" garden, Skylands in Maine. The house and gardens of this 1925 American treasure were designed by two renowned architects: The house was designed by Duncan Candler, and the gardens were conceived by the great landscape architect Jens Jensen. Upon purchase of this hilltop place—eighty-plus acres, numerous buildings, and more than a mile of road—I became a caretaker of history, and I loved this new job. There was no grass to mow, yet acres of forest and moss to tend, and terraces and balconies of pink granite needing planted pots and statement ornamentation.

Skylands has taught me a great deal about a different kind of gardening. Everything is subtle, subdued. On Mount Desert Island, everything takes its orders from nature. The moss is there, but it needs the year of fallen leaves and pine needles to be carefully blown off for it to burgeon into an emerald ground cover. To keep the forest mighty and populated, trees need pruning to allow sunlight and air to help them grow strong and shapely. Gardens need to be placed where there is sunlight, and the soil must be amended with compost, seaweed, and nutrients. The gardener has to learn to cope

with extremes of weather and a short but quick season once the growing starts. And Skylands has also reinforced the necessity for careful garden planning—what to plant, when to plant, how much to plant—so that the house can be filled with plumes of *Cotinus* (smoke bush), myriad branches of lilacs, dozens of lilies, and hundreds of sunflowers when I am there. That is when the house is always full of guests, and dinner parties are planned, and the garden is my only go-to source.

At present my biggest garden project is Cantitoe Farm, my 150-acre property in Katonah, about fifty miles north of New York City. It is still a "work in progress," a landscape with flower gardens, farm animals, horses, vegetable gardens, and greenhouses. I bought the place in 2000 and intended it to be my "last garden." I do not know if that will be the case, but it is certainly my largest garden to date. Simply laid out, on land that is gently sloping from one end (south) to the other (north), and intersected with smallish streams, the property is about 50 percent woodland and 50 percent pastures, fields, and gardens. There is lots of space to express my landscape ideas and ideals—four miles of curvaceous carriage roads enable me to quickly traverse from one end to the other on foot, on horseback, or by truck. The biggest accomplishment so far has been the careful delineation of spaces, the planting of allées of trees as well as boxwood, and my inclination now to replant the woodlands with many groves of interesting indigenous trees and plants. I have planted masses of my favorite kinds of flowers: a giant bed of pink-colored peonies; a very large perennial garden filled with

At Katonah, New York, Kevin Sharkey puts his cutting and arranging skills to work. Here, many varieties of freshly cut lilac boughs are gathered in collecting containers of water, carefully positioned in the back of the fully loaded Kawasaki Mule.

all of my favorite lilies, poppies, and irises, among hundreds of others; two long gardens filled with many kinds of lilac shrubs; and borders of hydrangeas, Japanese maple trees, clematis, shade plants, and tulip beds.

There is no lack of flowers at the farm for arranging and enjoying, and no shortage of incredible opportunities to plant more of everything. I have become more interested now in variety, more picky with color choices, more critical of each and every thing I have nurtured, wanting each plant to be healthy, each flower to be usable, and the gardens to be a constant source of inspiration to others, notably Kevin Sharkey.

Kevin came to work at *Martha Stewart Living,* the magazine, in 1996. He and I became instant colleagues and instant friends. Bostonian by birth, Kevin was educated at Rhode Island School of Design. He began his career at Parish-Hadley, the renowned decorating firm in New York City. (During school he had interned at the Arnold Arboretum, where he became knowledgeable about trees and shrubs, especially lilacs.) His love of flowers grew as he decorated rooms in the homes of famous gardeners—Mrs. Vincent Astor, for one, and Mrs. Jock Whitney.

Walking through my gardens years ago, it became clear to both of us that I was the grower, and he was the cutter and arranger. It was as if I wrote the music, and he wrote the lyrics. We started our collaboration at Turkey Hill in Westport and then continued it in East Hampton, in Katonah, and in Seal Harbor, Maine. Kevin knows my gardens almost as well as I do, and he knows exactly what will please me, what will look good in the planned location, and what will not. When he ventures out into the landscape to pick and combine what I have grown into coherent "wholes," he creates beautiful arrangements that fit the spaces allocated, the season, and the occasion.

Over the last two decades, we have learned a lot about each other—and flowers. Together we often plan the types of flowers we will plant in a new garden, and we have concocted beautiful gardening glossaries and articles for the magazine. I trust him with scissors in my garden like I trust no other, except for my daughter, Alexis.

The bouquets and arrangements in this book resulted from our close planning and envisioning—and luck—in growing spectacular blooms that combine well with one another, or with foliage, to bedazzle a room or call one's eyes to attention.

We are thrilled with the result of our labor, and hope you will be too.

And my motto for this book remains the same as in my first gardening book: *Pour l'avenir,* from the French, meaning "For the future."

Signs of Spring

For any gardener, spring is most likely the favorite time of the year. Certainly that is true for me in my Katonah garden. All the protective coverings from winter have been removed—the burlap wrapping the boxwood, the evergreen boughs blanketing the perennial beds from frost heaving, and the straw placed over outdoor, overwintering planters. The tender green leaves of azaleas and lilacs and the bright green shoots of all the bulbs and perennials emerge rapidly, day to day to day. Every bulb that was planted in the autumn is excitedly awaited, and the new varieties surprise and delight with their distinctive colors, shapes, and sizes.

Each year, I attempt to plant lots of new things and fill in where older specimens have weakened or died. One year, I will plant a bed of a few hundred tulips to try new types and singular offerings from my trusted suppliers, and I will be able to determine which will actually make it into some more permanent location. In the meantime, I have plenty to give as bouquets and to arrange for the house. And no matter how small the garden, there is always room for a few more fritillaria, a dozen or more blue *Muscari,* and some tender, tiny narcissus tucked into empty spaces among the later-blooming perennials.

SEASONAL
ALL-STARS

DAFFODIL
TULIP
RHODODENDRON
& AZALEA
LILAC
ALLIUM
PEONY

Woodland flowers such as lily of the valley, bluebells, and columbine herald the arrival of spring. But it's when the tulips bloom (here, 'Double Maureen', 'Barcelona', and 'Shirley') that the garden seems to fully wake from its winter calm and surge to life.

I am always surprised at how quickly the gardens turn from large, brownish, sad-looking areas into verdant, lush, even colorful tapestries of healthy, vibrant plants. There is lots to do in the garden in springtime, and it is best to keep a calendar, year to year, of exactly what is necessary to accomplish and what is planned, and which chores are to be done when. The calendar also acts as a record of when things bloom, how certain plants behave from year to year, and of surprises as they occur. I like to know, for example, when to expect the tree peonies, or the approximate dates the herbaceous peony garden blooms so that I can plan a dinner in celebration. My annual peony party has become something of a coveted and highly anticipated invitation among my friends and colleagues. Of course, all gardening zones differ in terms of when plants grow and bloom, and since my gardens are in the Northeast, my focus is there. But a calendar is terribly important to keep blooming, planting, and maintenance timelines in order.

Spring in Katonah begins in early March, when the first tiny bulbs start to bloom and the witch hazels bloom with yellow, red, orange, and rust-colored flowers. By Saint Patrick's Day, the edible peas are planted, and the gardens have been tilled and additional compost added where necessary. By the end of the month, the quince trees and forsythia will have bloomed and the ferns and hostas and other shade

LEFT: Bell-shaped fritillaria has a natural checkerboard pattern on petals that nod gracefully on the stem. Kevin emphasizes its shape in this ruby Venetian glass bottleneck vase, which works well with long-stemmed flowers.
RIGHT: Wood hyacinth (commonly known as bluebells) turns a spring wood into a scene from a fairy tale as it creates a natural blue carpet. In an arrangement, its unusual color and fluttery blossoms beg to be left alone, without another shade or shape to moderate it. An armload of these woodland flowers looks polished in a footed silver vessel.

plants will have grown large from their dormancy. The boxwood starts to green up, and the pastures and lawns turn deep emerald.

April is full of activity: The daffodil borders start blooming in earnest, and the flower gardens begin to look like gardens instead of forlorn spaces. All winter rubble, fallen twigs, and forgotten leaves are removed to make way for the new growth.

Late April and early May herald the apple blossoms, the unfurling of all the leaves on the trees, the lilacs starting to bloom, and the irises beginning to open. Wisteria, paulownia, pear, pawpaw, almond, and cherry trees dot the farm with fragrance and delicate blooms. That is, of course, if we do not have a damaging snow or ice storm that renders the fruit trees fruitless or freezes the wisteria blossoms. And the hellebores, in an amazing array of colors—from white to burgundy to almost black—bloom profusely.

May is the most glorious time at the farm. Tree peonies come into their exotic bloom first, followed by herbaceous peonies in their very own bed and in the cutting garden. The tulips start a monthlong growing cycle, planned carefully by planting early, midseason, and late bloomers. The wild orchids, lily of the valley, *Epimedium*, and all of the other important shade plants bloom and loom large everywhere.

And then, it starts to become warm as the days grow longer. Summer approaches.

Its distinctive petal shape makes columbine (*Aquilegia*) a star of spring arrangements. Rather than surround the flowers with a ring of green foliage, Kevin instead started with a center of lady's mantle (*Alchemilla*), studded the arrangement with leaves of the same plant, and then positioned golden columbine to form a cuff of butterfly-like flowers.

Spring is the season to celebrate flowering branches, like these pink-petaled beauties from the horse chestnut tree. The flower's golden interior is reflected in the choice of a warm brass bowl for this arrangement, accented with the tree's own foliage. As the flowers dry and fall, there's no need to sweep them away; they form a pool of blossoms that adds another element to the display. *OPPOSITE*: Here, Kevin combined hellebores in several shades in a large Venetian-glass vase, then added a grace note with a single stem in a smaller glass. A duplicate vessel stands alongside.

Using branches of fragrant magnolia cut at different heights, Kevin created a triangular shape in a silver pitcher, with buds jutting from the top right to give the arrangement pop. *OPPOSITE:* Embrace the movement of flowering forsythia by letting the branches sway in one direction. Here, a sheet of chicken wire acts as a frog, inserted into a wide Korean hibachi fitted with a metal liner. (To do this, cut a circle of chicken wire slightly larger than the diameter of your vessel, fold the edges under, and insert it just inside the top of the container.) Then, the center of the arrangement is built, starting with taller branches bent in the same direction and filling in with shorter stems around the edges. Forsythia has the added advantage of being voluminous on the tree, so there are plenty of branches available for cutting.

A solo daffodil or small grouping of blooms can offer just as much impact as a large bouquet, and leaves more of the flowers for you to enjoy in the garden. The small-scale display lets you appreciate the incredible form of the flower. Put a bloom in a bud vase or a flip glass with one of its own leaves, or place three or four flowers in a little ceramic pitcher. Cut their stems at different lengths for visual interest. Group a bunch of dwarf blooms (such as 'Tazetta', mixed with doubles and trumpets) together in a simple ceramic vessel.

Daffodil

NARCISSUS

ALL DAFFODILS—FROM BIG YELLOW TRUMPETS TO TINY ROCK-GARDEN DELICACIES, AND EVERYTHING IN BETWEEN— HAVE THREE ESSENTIAL CHARACTERISTICS THAT MAKE THEM THE ULTIMATE NO-FUSS PERENNIALS: DEER- AND OTHER PEST-PROOF QUALITIES, THE DESIRE TO BLOOM AND MULTIPLY, AND UNABASHED GOOD CHEER.

In Katonah, an area plagued by rampant deer, I originally planned to protect only small portions of my garden with fencing. After a few years of planting thousands of daffodils, boxwood, and shade-loving plants disliked by these large and always-hungry four-legged creatures, I decided to surround the entire 150 acres with an 8-foot fence. The fence has been a tremendous help in permitting me to plant pretty much anything I want, and new trees, shrubs, and flowers are undisturbed by the burgeoning deer population.

The best thing I did during those indecisive, pre-fence years, however, was to begin planting a long, wide daffodil border down one side of my property. That portion of the farm runs alongside Maple Avenue, a glorious dirt road lined with ancient maple trees, where many people hike, run, and walk their dogs.

At first I thought I would plant the bulbs outside the stone wall that borders all

the road frontage. There is a wide swath of grass outside the wall adjoining the road, and I believed I would be beautifying the neighborhood. When I discovered how much my first ten thousand daffodil bulbs were going to cost, I reconsidered and planted the entire ten thousand inside the wall where I could actually see them, smell them, and enjoy them up close!

Choosing bulbs for naturalizing requires a great deal of research and ultimately experimentation. I called my friends at Brent and Becky's Bulbs in Virginia to discuss their most successful naturalizers, or perennializers, as Brent calls bulbs that will continually grow and multiply and flower year after year. I also conferred with the folks at Van Engelen in Connecticut, who were very helpful in steering me toward bulbs that would grow well in Westchester County.

Then I immersed myself in the methods of planting thousands of bulbs and came up with the useful practice of preparing a low area in the garden, laying the bulbs out en masse, and covering them with amended soils. I find this so much easier than digging individual holes, which becomes extremely tiring after the first hundred or so bulbs.

For the most part, the daffodil borders (I have now planted more than just the Maple Avenue border) are wonderful—colorful, long lived, and useful for cut flowers. Over the years, I have planted more than sixty thousand daffodils on the property, and each spring I invite my daughter and a small group of friends to pick handfuls of their favorites. Not all the naturalizing types are great for arranging, but all are beautiful in bloom, and those that cut well and have longevity as cut flowers are invaluable additions to any garden.

A note to the decorative gardener: Daffodils are best planted alone, in masses, in places where they can be enjoyed in early spring but that are not in full view all year long. Daffodil foliage requires a long period of drying after the blooms disappear, and that portion of your garden is best left alone until the dried foliage can be removed. Also, feeding before and after blooming helps with bulb naturalizing and multiplication.

Naturalized daffodils at the farm are massed fairly close together in clusters of the same variety—about twenty varieties among three thousand daffodils. Make sure when you're naturalizing to choose an area that has good drainage and receives some sun. Early-blooming cultivars can be planted at the edge of a wood, as they will receive enough sun to ripen the foliage before the trees mature their own foliage. Also choose an area where the grass can be left unmowed until foliage has matured.

GROWING
& ARRANGING

THE DISTINCT ADVANTAGE TO PLANTING MASSES OF DAFFODILS
INSTEAD OF OTHER BULBS, SUCH AS TULIPS AND HYACINTHS,
IS THAT THEY ARE A DETERRENT TO DEER AND RODENTS. A BORDER
OF TULIPS COULD BE COMPLETELY DESTROYED BY HUNGRY DEER,
BUT DAFFODILS? THEY SHOULD LAST FOR YEARS IN YOUR GARDEN.

HOW TO GROW

When choosing daffodils, plant some early bloomers (*Narcissus* 'Rijnveld's Early Sensation', 'February Gold'), midseason bloomers ('Ice Wings', 'Katie Heath'), and late bloomers ('Intrigue', *N. poeticus* var. *recurvus*). That way, you can stretch the season to six or eight weeks—or even longer.

ZONE *Narcissus* grows in a wide range of zones, often from Zones 4 or 5 through Zones 7 or 8, but many tolerate as cold as Zone 3 or as warm as Zone 9. Check specific plant descriptions if you live in one of the extremes.

SOIL *Narcissus* can tolerate most soils as long as the drainage is good. Hillsides and raised beds are your best options. If the composition of your soil leans toward clay, improve it with well-rotted compost, soil amendment, or planting mix, and raise the bed. Slightly acidic soil is best, so consider adding soil sulfur if you have alkaline soil.

LIGHT Daffodils prefer exposure to the sun at least half of the day, and can tolerate partial shade. The exceptions are pink-cupped varieties, which thrive in partial shade (full sun bleaches them out).

CHOOSING Since you can plant bulbs right up to the time the soil is frozen, you can take advantage of late-season bulb sales. When you purchase bulbs, discard any with signs of white or pink fungus (they may have narcissus basal rot). Choose bulbs that are firm and have retained their papery layers, with tips that have not sprouted. Select a mix of heights, flower types, and bloom times.

PLANTING Autumn is the time to plant daffodils. The plants grow roots in the fall, once the soil temperature at the depth of the bulb falls below 60 degrees (this occurs well after the first frost). Roots stop growing once the ground freezes, then restart in the spring when the soil thaws.

Plant the bulbs with the pointed end up, at a depth three to four times the height of the bulb. Amend the soil with bone meal, superphosphate, and rich compost if needed. For a large plot, apply the fertilizer and then forkdig to a depth of 8 inches. If you're planting bulbs in individual holes, sprinkle fertilizer in each hole and mix well. It's important to make sure that the fertilizer doesn't touch the bulb directly or it will burn it.

Daffodil plantings should feel natural, not "gardened." (See Naturalizing Daffodils, page 35.) Mass them fairly close together in clusters of the same variety (against deciduous trees or evergreen shrubs, or tucked among ground cover). Or toss them onto the prepared ground, planting them where they fall.

To make planting easier, consider using a bulb planter instead of a trowel. Daffodils can also grow in containers as long as there is room to multiply, and for the roots to fill out. They can bloom well in containers for one to two years—after that, it's best to move them to a spot in the ground.

WATERING Give daffodils plenty of water after planting, during bloom, and while the

An unused bocce court—8 inches below the level of the shade garden—proved to be the perfect site for naturalizing daffodils. Finding an existing hollow or depressed area in your garden allows you to use the "no-dig" method of planting. Create a plan and map it out in the soil (see Naturalizing Daffodils, page 35). For the three thousand bulbs we planted, we used granular lime to demarcate small sections that would each hold twenty-five to fifty bulbs (depending on the size), laid them all out at once, and then covered the entirety with soil and compost.

foliage is still green. Gradually decrease watering as the flowers fade and the leaves begin to turn yellow, and stop completely when they turn brown and dry (seasonal rain should give them the water they need).

FERTILIZING If the daffodil display begins to slow down after a few years, a fall application of slow-release, potassium-rich fertilizer (such as 10:10:20) may improve things. Top-dress with bulb booster and potash (just before a rain, if possible) in the fall and then just as the shoots are emerging from the ground in spring.

PRUNING Daffodils never require dividing, never need deadheading, and should never have their foliage cut, braided, or wrapped with rubber bands to appear neater. That foliage has to be fully exposed to sunlight to supply enough energy for next year's display and for the bulbs to multiply. Until the leaves go yellow, they are hard at work. Unsightly foliage is better dealt with through clever planting combinations—plant daffodils with perennials, annuals, or even vegetables that will grow tall enough or leaf out sufficiently to hide dying foliage. Once brown and dry, foliage can be removed.

TROUBLESHOOTING Overall, daffodils are low-maintenance and generally worry-free: Animals don't eat them (their bulbs are poisonous and have an unattractive flavor to rodents and deer), diseases and pests are rare, and they don't require much—if any—regular maintenance. However, yellow to white striped leaves or dead tips can indicate a virus; simply dig up and discard any affected plants. Pests such as the narcissus bulb fly are rare but something to be aware of; if you have any issues with them, try mowing or cutting the leaves back in late spring to discourage the pests.

Just because daffodils have a limited spectrum of petal hues (they come in shades of yellow, white, orange, and pink) doesn't mean you can't make a bold color statement. Use one type of daffodil in several variations, such as the large cup and trumpet forms seen here, to create a yellow-on-yellow arrangement. Arrange the flowers in color order, moving from light to dark to build an ombré effect. Daffodils aren't especially tall flowers, so don't look to them for soaring arrangements. Instead, place them in a bubble bowl or mixing bowl that complements their profile and allows the color effects of the flower heads to make the impact.

OPPOSITE: Daffodils are wonderful on their own, but they actually play well with the shapes and colors of their sister spring-garden blooms. Here, daffodil trumpets ('Quail', 'Professor Einstein', and 'Delibes') meet fiery-orange and pale-yellow tulips, delicate white lily of the valley, viburnum, and lady's mantle.

Just remember before mixing them with other flowers to let daffodil stems drain in lukewarm water so that the toxic sap dissipates (see page 35). Play with informal vessels, too. Add texture such as a woven willow basket or a galvanized bucket for a kitchen or outdoor display.

CUTTING The weather can affect the longevity of these spring flowers. Whereas cool, cloudy days help preserve a bed of blooms for up to three weeks, one hot, sunny afternoon may cause them to fade overnight. To prevent the weather from wreaking havoc on daffodils at bloom time, cut the flowers in the morning and use them for indoor arrangements. Daffodils harvested when the buds are tightly closed and still green will keep well in a vase for up to a week. Before arranging them, condition thoroughly by letting the stems soak in tepid water. The freshly cut ends emit crystals of calcium oxalate, an irritant that may shorten their life and poison other flowers in the arrangement. Change the water every few minutes until the thick sap no longer appears, at which point the daffodils are safe to combine with other blossoms.

ARRANGING Because they're not especially tall flowers, a bubble bowl works well for daffodils. Kevin appreciates the beauty of the green stems, so he prefers to use a clear glass vessel. Galvanized metal buckets and wicker baskets are good informal choices. Use the daffodils in a bunch or with other spring favorites (lilacs and tulips) when the color palette is right. If you mix varieties of daffodils, keep the scale in mind, as well as the composition of the blossoms and the color.

NATURALIZING DAFFODILS

Growing naturalistic clusters and drifts of the flowers can fill in your property where it's a bit bare. Daffodils look beautiful along a gray stone wall, sprinkled in a yet-to-be-leafed out woodland, dotted on a hillside, and nestled next to apple trees. In Katonah, we have tens of thousands of daffodils along one of the borders of the farm, and we created a large garden bed of three thousand daffodil bulbs. Here's a practical guide to doing it yourself:

1. **DRAW THE PLAN FOR YOUR BED.** Using a bulb catalog as a guide, make a planting scheme that arranges each daffodil variety in groups, or "drifts," of colors, heights, and blooming times.

2. **PREPARE THE BED AND MAP IT OUT.** For larger plantings, use a no-dig method. Look for a natural depression or hollow on your property where you can place the bulbs 8 inches below ground level. Or, in smaller flowerbeds, remove the top layer of soil to the proper planting depth. Scatter bulb fertilizer or amendments such as bone meal over the area and work in. Mark the plan directly on the soil surface with lime.

3. **POSITION THE BULBS.** Place each bulb root flat-side down, and space them 2 to 6 inches apart in a loose grid. Avoid military-style straight lines to achieve the most naturalized effect.

4. **COVER THEM UP.** Fill in with topsoil and compost, raking until the surface is flat (avoid stepping on the surface).

5. **CHOOSE WISELY.** Among the many varieties planted at my farm, here are seven standouts:

- 'Barrett Browning': White with rich orange cups; 14 to 16 inches (midseason bloomers).
- 'Flower Record': White petals and yellow cups edged with orange; 18 to 20 inches (midseason to late).
- 'Ice Follies': White with butter-yellow cups; 16 to 20 inches (midseason).
- 'Mount Hood': Wide, creamy-yellow trumpets; 16 to 20 inches (midseason).
- 'Thalia': Pure white star-shaped flowers, often two flowers per stem; 14 to 18 inches (midseason).
- 'Yellow Cheerfulness': The pure yellow version of 'Cheerfulness'; 14 to 16 inches (late).
- 'Martha Stewart': Plant breeder Karel van der Veek honored me by creating this late-blooming daffodil, exclusive to Van Engelen bulb suppliers, with delicate white petals and a yellow cup with frilled peach edges.

Don't overlook grass when arranging daffodils—or other flowers. It can work with the flower's own slender stem to add a touch of green. Here, in an Edwardian-era pressed-glass trumpet vase, the long, curvy lines of grass from the farm's pasture complement the graceful shape of 'Hawera' narcissus, a triandrus type (with two or more tiny pale-yellow blossoms on each stem). Grasses like these help to provide movement within an arrangement—the flower stems standing upright, the grasses bending at will—without crowding the blooms.

Beyond familiar yellows, there are so many creamy-colored daffodils to love, including 'Accent', with an apricot-colored cup, the pink split-cupped 'Palmares', the pink-rimmed 'Elizabeth Ann', and the pure white 'Thalia'. Similar varieties include 'Salome', 'Precocious', and 'Candy Princess'. Their dark stems intertwine and are visible in this glass apothecary jar, offering a frothy mix of blooms above a rich green base.

OPPOSITE: If you're going big, go all out. A vessel like this tower of cones holds a half dozen yellow and white varieties (including 'Fortune', 'Actaea', 'Primeur', 'Fortissimo', and 'Arkle') at once, each with its own space to shine. This is the opposite of the low-key, one-bloom strategy, and best for an occasion when you want to make a strong statement. It also works on a shorter scale—put a different variety of daffodil in each of several low vases, arranged down a table.

Single, double, peony, fringed, and parrot-style tulips including 'Bleu Aimable', 'Blue Spectacle' (a double-form purple), 'Formosa' (yellow), 'Flaming Parrot' (red and yellow variegated), 'Black Parrot' (dark ruffled), and 'Queen of Night' are combined in a vintage cast-iron brazier in a faux-bamboo pattern. "This is one of my favorite compositions," says Kevin. "Martha suggested that I create something bold and outrageous, and this was the result." A color palette of rosy purples and pops of yellow allows the eye to appreciate the vast array of flower shapes available within the tulip family. To assemble, Kevin used tulips in full bloom, with a few lilac stems as accents. The stems are allowed to bend and bubble over the brazier's edge.

Tulip

TULIPA

PROBABLY NO OTHER FLOWER HAS ENGENDERED AS MUCH CURIOSITY, INTEREST, AND ROMANTIC INTRIGUE AS THE TULIP. THESE SMOOTH, SILKY-TO-THE-TOUCH BULBS, MEMBERS OF THE LILY FAMILY, HAVE MADE FORTUNES FOR BOTANISTS, CAUSED INTERNATIONAL SCANDALS, AND CHANGED THE WAY WE PLANT, AND LOOK AT, SPRINGTIME GARDENS.

I have been growing these graceful, colorful, easy-to-grow flowers forever, it seems. My fondness for which colors to plant changes from year to year, depending on where in my garden I want to invest my energies with hundreds of gorgeous tulips—sometimes in a single color, sometimes in a mix of varying shades, sizes, and types.

One year, in a rush to grow sufficient tulips for photographing, I ordered fifty of each tulip that caught my fancy while studying the Brent and Becky's Bulbs catalog. We planted several thousand in a large, well-prepared bed just next to my cutting garden. Each type of bulb had its own row, and each row was numbered and cataloged on a map for future reference. I had never planted quite so many tulips in one place and the experiment was amazing. We made so many arrangements of cut tulips, gave so many as gifts, and learned so much about the growing habits of many different types.

"I HAVE A PENCHANT FOR SMALL SPRING FLOWERS AND MANY TULIP VARIETIES FIT THIS CATEGORY—KAUFMANNIANA, FOSTERIANA, GREIGII, CLUSIANA, AND BAKERI, TO NAME A FEW."

The "en masse" planting method has been the favored way to show tulips in gardens for several hundred years, but now many gardeners have forsaken tradition and instead plant tulips loosely here and there amid perennial plants, in azalea borders, and among beds of soft, low-growing plants such as *Alchemilla*. By choosing colors and types wisely, these planting methods can really enhance the early-spring garden, and tulips can bloom over a period exceeding six weeks.

The catalog descriptions of the different kinds of tulips are fascinating, but I can assure you that almost every type is valuable as a cut flower: Tulips range from very tall and elegant to much shorter and sturdy. In the latter category are the single early and double early. The Triumph group are midseason, of medium height, and last a long time in arrangements. The midseason bloomers of the Darwin hybrid group are tall, graceful, and very desirable as cut flowers, with huge blooms and spectacular colors. The single late types allow for extended bloom time. They have long stems, come in beautiful hues, and are also very good cut flowers; their petals can be lily-shaped, scalloped, flamed, or striped. Fringed tulips are midseason or late, single or double, and medium to tall in height. And then there are 'Viridiflora', single-flowered cultivars whose petals all have some green on them. They are especially hardy in the garden and are excellent in arrangements. The 'Parrot' tulips are single-flowered cultivars, medium to tall, with huge flowers in vivid single or multiple colors. I especially love 'Flaming Parrot', a red and yellow tulip that can grow 27 inches tall!

Lastly, for cut flowering types, are the very popular double late, or peony-flowered, tulips. They are long-stemmed late bloomers. The most popular of this type have been 'Angelique', a pale pink, and 'Mount Tacoma', an ivory white.

Of course, many other tulips, and types of tulips, are available to American growers. I have a penchant for small spring flowers and many tulip varieties fit this category—*kaufmanniana, fosteriana, greigii, clusiana,* and *bakeri,* to name a few. I suggest that you gather suppliers' catalogs and sit and pick and choose, as I do. Order in late summer or very early fall to be sure you get what you want. And plant as soon as you receive the bulbs, so they have time to start the growing process before the very cold winter months.

Tulips are not like daffodils; they do not necessarily bloom year to year, but with proper care you can prolong some of your initial investment. That first year after planting is the one that requires documentation, including photographs, and parties so you can invite others to observe the "Tulipomania" taking place in your own garden.

Mounted on the side of the Winter House at the farm in Katonah, this American folk art wrought-iron wall stand normally holds plants; using it to display different bunches of flowers illustrates the abundance of the cutting garden. Here, fourteen of the varieties from my tulip beds at Katonah greet guests as they arrive at the height of spring. Varieties include 'Apricot Parrot', 'Hakuun', 'Spring Green', 'Jackpot', 'Helmar', 'Cashmir', 'Purple Prince', 'Monsella', 'Weber's Parrot', and 'Angelique'.

GROWING
& ARRANGING

TULIPS (TULIPA) HAVE BEEN GROWN AROUND THE WORLD
FOR CENTURIES. IN FACT, THEY WERE SO COVETED
DURING THE HEIGHT OF "TULIPOMANIA" IN SEVENTEENTH-
CENTURY HOLLAND THAT A SINGLE BULB COULD COST AS
MUCH AS A HOUSE. TODAY THERE ARE MORE THAN
THREE THOUSAND GARDEN VARIETIES TO CHOOSE FROM.

HOW TO GROW

The best thing about growing tulips is how undemanding they are. Different varieties bloom at different times, so by judiciously mixing cultivars from early-, middle-, and late-season classes, you can have tulips in bloom for six weeks or more. When I lived in Westport, Connecticut, I tucked clusters of bulbs wherever there was space among the perennials and shrubs; now, at the farm in Katonah, I have an entire bed of my cutting garden dedicated to these beautiful flowers.

ZONE Most tulips thrive in Zones 3 to 8, which means they grow readily everywhere from the Dakotas to the mid-South in the United States, though they tend to fare better in the cooler zones, up to Zone 7. They can even bloom in the Deep South and Southwest, Zones 8 to 10, as long as they're treated like annuals and the bulbs are refrigerated for six to ten weeks before planting (see Chilling, page 45). In many areas with warmer winters, bulbs are often sold prechilled. This simulates the winter freeze and thawing process that encourages bulbs to spring into action.

SOIL Sandy soil enriched with organic matter works best for tulips; they also need good drainage and prefer a pH level of 6.0 to 6.5. Prepare the soil by adding compost and bulb booster, a fertilizer made especially for

bulbs, and use a garden fork to loosen the soil to the depth you will be planting—which should be quite deep, about 8 inches below the surface. Aerated soil will allow the plants to grow strong, healthy roots.

LIGHT Plant tulips in full sun, unless you are growing varieties with dark (or even black) blossoms—these petals can burn in constant sun, so a little shade is preferable.

CHOOSING Watch for mold on bulbs. To test a bulb, immerse it in water. Healthy bulbs should sink, while those with decay will float. Also ensure the bulb has retained its outer covering (tunic), which can slip off easily.

PLANTING Plant tulips in the middle of fall, or as soon as they arrive from the supplier. You can plant tulips, like daffodils, right up until the soil freezes, so if you get a late start, take advantage of end-of-season bulb sales.

You can plant tulips in informal clusters, or take a cue from the tulip fields of Holland and plant varieties in straight lines or distinct blocks. You can also space clusters close together in a container—a few bulbs each in 6- to 8-inch diameter pots with plenty of drainage holes. Cover the pots with wire screening to keep out vermin that love to gnaw on the bulbs. Be sure to plant the area all at once to avoid digging into an already-planted bulb;

On the farm in Katonah, the tulip beds (located in what was once the pumpkin patch) comprise three thousand bulbs arranged in neat rows— a smaller-scale version of the famed Dutch tulip fields. We arrange varieties according to color, height, and bloom time. The cutting beds are situated such that the flowers enjoy full sun throughout the summer, in a dry area of the garden.

in large plots, mark your layout with bone meal. Always plant bulbs at a depth of three times their height and at least 8 inches deep; in areas with squirrels, deer, and rabbits, try a depth of four times the bulb height. This is also a good trick in regions with frequent freezing and thawing, to prevent heaving (when roots are pushed to the surface due to the freezing and thawing action of the soil).

Bulb planters—tools that feature a long metal cylinder with a handle—are extremely efficient for planting tulips; pick one up at a garden or home center. The tool neatly cuts and removes a section of soil, allowing for the bulb to be dropped in, the soil replaced, and the planting completed in just a few steps.

WATERING Water the bulbs regularly throughout spring, but gradually discontinue watering for the summer. Most tulips prefer to stay dry to mimic the conditions of their native habitat. Once they are established and have begun flowering, normal rainfall should suffice, unless the season is unnaturally dry. Never water from above while the tulips are in bud or bloom, as water on the petals can cause burning, spots, and shattering.

FERTILIZING At planting time, feed tulips by mixing bulb fertilizer (follow product instructions for dosage) into the soil at the bottom of the deep planting hole. Feed again in the spring, and continue to fertilize established plantings each fall. In Katonah, the tulip beds receive a generous dose of bulb food and bone meal before planting, before the first snowfall, and again in the early spring before shoots emerge. We also treat with an extra layer of compost each year in the fall.

PRUNING Deadheading tulips is necessary to prevent the plant from wasting energy on developing seed capsules. Simply cut off fading flowers below the swollen bases. You can also cut any bare stem below the seed capsules, but leave the foliage on the plant until it yellows and browns. The yellowing leaves are necessary to help fuel next year's bloom cycle. If you prefer to hide withering foliage, mix in other perennials for ground cover. If any older bulbs fail to bloom or bloom poorly, pull them so that they can be replaced the next fall. Be sure to keep tulip beds weeded during summer.

CHILLING In warmer regions (Zones 8 to 10), where the soil doesn't stay below 50 degrees long enough to give the tulips a cold period, you will need to purchase prechilled bulbs or store bulbs in a dry, cool place, such as the bottom shelf of the refrigerator or an empty root cellar. Place the bulbs away from fruits and vegetables, which produce ethylene gas that can harm the embryonic flowers inside the bulbs. Make sure the bulbs remain dry. The usual chilling time is ten weeks or longer at 40 to 45 degrees. Once the bulbs are removed from cold treatment, plant them right away. Bloom occurs about six to eight weeks after planting. Though the simulated chilling period will lead to blooms the first few years, you may begin to notice declining quality by the third year, depending on the variety. The flowers will eventually start to exhibit the effects of not receiving a true winter ground freeze, and you will likely need to start afresh with new bulbs.

TROUBLESHOOTING Tulip bulbs are irresistible to squirrels and deer. Plant tulip bulbs alongside daffodils or crown imperial (*Fritillaria imperialis*)—these bulbs have an unpleasant flavor and may help keep vermin away. You can also bury sheets of chicken wire (with openings no bigger than 1 inch wide) in the soil just above newly planted bulbs. Stems and foliage will easily grow through the mesh, but squirrels and deer should be prevented from reaching the bulbs. Place chicken wire just below the bulbs for extra protection—or plant groups of bulbs in wire cages (available at hardware stores).

Other methods include sprinkling bulbs with cayenne pepper or sprinkling the ground above the bulbs with bone meal as a rodent deterrent. The best way to keep deer out is with a good fence specifically manufactured to be deer-resistant. Deer repellent is less efficient: it doesn't always work and needs to be reapplied often.

Because tulips are planted individually, diseased or problematic bulbs can be removed easily. If you notice spindly stems and white or yellowish mottling or streaking of the foliage, your tulips may have a virus or blight. Simply dig up and remove the entire bulb before it spreads. If you see aphids on your tulips, spray them with water.

Single- and double-variety tulips bloom in the garden. Van Engelen's 'Apricot Parrot', top left, is a May bloomer with beautiful fringed petals. At top right, 'Orange Princess' tulips are Rembrandt-type midspring bloomers with a stronger fragrance than some others. 'Monte Carlo', bottom, has fully double, bright yellow cups, and is a good choice for beds, forcing, and arrangements.

CUTTING You can harvest tulips when the buds are still predominantly green, with a touch of color starting to show, though many florists—and Kevin—prefer to cut them in full bloom, to ensure they open to the desired degree. If there is a leaf (or two) on the upper part of the stem, leave it intact if possible—it will encourage the blossom to fully open and hold its shape better by increasing light intake. Always cut flowers in the morning and place them in cold water.

MAINTAINING Place tulips in cool spaces out of direct sunlight to avoid burning the petals, and change the water regularly. When kept in clean, plentiful water, some varieties, especially parrot tulips, can last up to two weeks. Tulips are notorious for growing, or "jumping," in the vase after cutting. An important trick (one Kevin recommends) is to "slit the throat" by using a pin or small knife to pierce the neck of the tulip stem, right below the blossom. This allows the stem to release oxygen so that the cut flower doesn't continue to grow. Even after slitting the throat, tulips will often flop over in arrangements. If you want to keep them straight, try putting them in a tall bucket right after cutting, so the heads are below the rim and contained. You can also

BLOOM TYPES

There are more than five hundred tulip cultivars registered with the Netherland Royal General Bulbgrowers' Association, a group of more than 1,200 growers and companies around the world. Over the years, breeders have pushed the tulip in a number of different directions, with each bloom category differing in the stature of the plant and the form of the flower—from the simple traditional tulip shape to pointed-petal lilies and showy peony or parrot forms.

SINGLE TULIPS are cup-shaped, with one bloom per stem and six petals, and come in early-, mid-, or late-flowering varieties. My single varieties include 'Hakuun', a midspring white and cream hybrid; 'Shirley', an ivory bloom with purple edges that fade to rosy blush in maturity; 'Maureen', a late-blooming oval-shaped white variety; 'Queen of Night', a velvety maroon that veers toward black; 'Spring Green', with ivory and apple-green feathered petals; 'Negrita', a midspring bloomer in reddish purple; 'Princess Irene', a Rembrandt-type orange-and-purple–flamed variety; and my Emperor tulips, including the unusual and elegant green and white 'Exotic', a pure heirloom white that can bloom for more than twenty years, and the bright pop of 'Orange Emperor'. My lily-form tulips also fall under this category, with graceful, pointed petals on tall stems, such as 'Formosa', a brilliant yellow with green streaks.

DOUBLE TULIPS usually have twelve or more petals, sometimes with a fluffy appearance and tall stems. In Katonah, we grow 'Monsella', an exuberant yellow-and-red–streaked variety with a strong fragrance and long-lasting flowers; 'Mondial', a white and green variety attractive to pollinators; and many others that fall into their own subcategories, such as 'Blue Spectacle', a peony-form tulip with many layers of showy, blue-leaning purple petals.

PARROT TULIPS are my favorite category, with ruffled petals that bring an elegant showiness to the tulip beds and contrast nicely against the crisp lines of more traditional forms. They can be single or double, usually bloom in May, and are named for the bud's resemblance to a parrot beak. Some of my parrot varieties grown include 'Blondine', a rare pale-yellow cultivar feathered with spring green and rose colors; 'Bleu Aimable', a tall purple bloom with gently ruffled petals and a white and blue center; 'Salmon Parrot', with its scalloped edges and pink, green, and yellow color; 'Blue Parrot', a bluish-bronze–tinged violet bloom; 'Black Parrot', a dark-burgundy heirloom with nearly black accents; and 'Flaming Parrot', a yellow and blood-red bloom with especially strong stems that are great for arranging.

FRINGED TULIPS can be single or double blooms that flower late in the season, with fringed or heavily ruffled petal edges, sometimes in contrasting colors. 'Cool Crystal', a fringed and peony hybrid grown at the farm, boasts strawberry and cream hues and showy, fluffy heads.

In the greenhouse at Cantitoe Corners, Kevin gathered these red 'Cashmir' and yellow 'Fringed Elegance' tulips in the farm's signature metal buckets. (A Chinese stoneware storage jar in front awaits an arrangement.) The red and yellow tulips play off each other and the marbleized 'Monsella' and 'Caribbean Parrot' varieties nicely. I use my greenhouse to grow hothouse tropical plants, but it also makes a wonderful staging area for arrangements before they're brought into the main house. At far right, 'Formosa' tulips show off their yellow and green-flamed petals.

wrap them tightly in newspaper after cutting, and place the entire bundle in water.

ARRANGING Older, more developed tulips are the most likely to bend—no matter which tricks you utilize. When you have a bending tulip, try using it as an element of movement within the architecture of the arrangement. Consider the horizontal gesture the tulip blossoms will create, and fill in the center with other upright blooms so they don't leave empty spaces behind. Tulips are, of course, beautiful on their own, but can also be lovely in arrangements combined with lilacs, fritillaria, and different kinds of foliage, such as rhubarb leaves. Restrict yourself to a narrow palette by grouping flowers in shades of the same color family, or embrace the multitude of colors available, like a Dutch tulip field. I love to pair orange and black, or arrange white, yellow, and mauve tulips together. Kevin often opts for pink and yellow pairings.

Almost any container can be used for tulip arrangements. Their good-looking stems can handle a clear glass vase or cut crystal; arrange a bunch together in a pail for a rustic display, or embrace the contrasting texture of a woven basket. Kevin's go-to vessels for tulips are trumpet vases, which encourage the movement and shape of the stems, and ginger jars. For an unusual approach, Kevin likes to cut off the tulip heads and perch them in shot glasses, so they look like colorful eggs in cups.

The slender English blown-glass trumpet vase used for this arrangement of tulips celebrates the natural structure of the flower, letting the stems, blossoms, and foliage do all the work. "The character of a tulip is so beautiful on its own," Kevin says. "It can handle unconventional foliage." Here, *Ligularia* leaves lend a dark, dramatic accent to the deep purple of 'Black and White' tulips.

Neatly trimmed tulip stems can stand up under observation in a shallow glass mantel vase like this one, which holds a mix of tulips, white bleeding hearts (*Dicentra*), and the wavy leaves of Japanese bird's nest fern. Kevin used the curving *Dicentra* to create the illusion of movement, allowing it to arc out and away from the center of the bouquet. The deep green of the ferns provides a perfect background against which the white 'Double Maureen' tulips can pop: together with the purple and white 'Jackpot' variety, they are a stabilizing presence for the airy arrangement.

Different hues can happily coexist in an arrangement without being deliberately integrated or mixed together. Here, 'Jan Reus' tulips (dark crimson single-blossoms), 'Ballerina' (lily-flowered blooms with crimson-edged petals), and 'Perestroyka' (a large, lily-shaped variety in pale orange flushed with pink) are grouped alongside fritillaria, primrose, wallflower, and ivy. In a footed vase, they are permitted to splay outward in every direction. *OPPOSITE:* On a counter at the Tenant House in Katonah, a modest arrangement of 'Caribbean Parrot' variegated tulips in an ironstone mixing bowl is elevated by a decorative wooden platform, lending balance to the arrangement and establishing a heftier presence. Kevin used a tape grid across the mouth of this bowl in order to stabilize the short-stemmed flowers; it also has the benefit of making an arrangement look like it has more flowers than it actually does. This low display is perfect as a kitchen table centerpiece, so guests can see one another over the top.

By a window in the Tenant House, simple tulip cuttings show off every angle and height this flower can offer. An arrangement series like this one, featuring 'Blue Spectacle' and 'Bleu Aimable' tulips, in late-1920s McCoy pottery, illustrates the idea that the sum of many flower types can be greater than its individual parts; when used in combination, an asymmetrical trumpet, a bursting bubble bowl, and a freeform tangle of stems balance and complement one another. A single blossom in a fingerbowl completes the tableau.

OPPOSITE: Purple tulips lend drama to a late-spring bouquet that would delight any of the Dutch master painters with its varying textures and deep colors. Varieties including 'Queen of Night', a very dark-purple single tulip, dark-purple 'Greuze', roselike 'Lilac Perfection', feathery-fringed 'Black Parrot', and white-edged 'Arabian Mystery' are paired with fritillaria, lilacs, and rhubarb and *Heuchera* foliage. Though small, fritillaria can add a great deal of impact to an arrangement, with its graceful stems and distinctly patterned, delicately pointed blossoms.

Green goes with everything in the garden, making it easy to pair with accent colors. The pink and yellow parrot tulips in this arrangement pair nicely with the pretty geranium leaves, viburnum, and fritillaria. To build an arrangement like this, start with a tape grid (see page 262), then add the tallest stems in the center and work toward the rim. To hide the tape, tuck in the outermost ring of flowers and foliage at a steep angle. For an unexpected touch, Kevin turned back some of the tulip petals to modify their form. *OPPOSITE*: On a wicker table, I arranged tulips and lilacs in a McCoy ceramic vase. "This represents a riot of the season," says Kevin. Yet every spring bloom doesn't have to result in a chaotic bouquet: stick to a limited color palette, like the blush ivories and whites here, and let the natural green of the garden be your accent color. The cloudlike blooms are brought down to earth by using the woven surface, showing how the textures of an arrangement's surroundings and backdrop can be incorporated to great effect.

KEVIN SHARKEY

Tulips can look very severe and very modern, or they can look very lush and romantic. They can truly do it all.

What are some of your favorite varieties?

I love parrot tulips, and my favorites are the 'Black Parrot' variety. I love the form of the flower—they're reckless and savage and have so much movement. You can create great foundational arrangements with them because they have such strong stems. But I also like the lily varieties, which are the total opposite shape, with very severe and angular petals. My new favorite is a marbleized, or "broken," tulip, the 'Black and White', available from Old House Gardens. It's a really old, rare variety, and it's so unusual, it actually stopped me in my tracks in the Katonah garden. 'Insulinde' and 'Absalon' are other marbleized varieties.

What do you love about them?

The fragrance is amazing. When I'm arranging certain flowers, like lilacs, I can appreciate the scent for a while and then I get so used to it that I no longer notice. And with something heady like lilies, the scent is so overwhelming that it's kind of like getting drunk too fast. Smelling a tulip is an intentional action, however, and it just makes something magical happen. You have to put your head right into the tulip in order to get the fragrance, and it's so individual to this flower.

How do you cut tulips?

I like to cut long stems, but Martha wants to make sure the bulb stays strong for next year, which means not removing as much of the stem. She cuts tulips at a reasonable length, maybe 12 inches, but I like to cut them all the way down to the ground. I think the construction of the blossom is really balanced best by a long stem. Martha instinctively takes into consideration how much to leave behind so that the bulb will replenish itself. She's thinking about the future of her cutting garden, but I'm all about what it looks like in that moment.

How do you like to pair them?

I like lilacs with tulips, and I like foliage. I especially like tulips with other tulips—you're able to see each tulip more clearly because they are such a simple shape; your eye might look for other shapes and they just aren't there, which allows for a better appreciation of the main flower.

Any special considerations?

You just have to be aware of the dirt and sand hidden beneath the leaves. Tulips can be deceiving because the stem looks clean once the leaves are off, but generally there's sand and dirt left behind, and you need to make sure you have a clean stem. You can use any sharp, small knife to clean it out.

Right after cutting a tulip, I slit the throat of it, a trick I learned when I was working for a florist. This way, when I'm arranging, I'm not spending a ton of time primping each flower. It's part of the prep, kind of like what a sous chef would do: choose leaves, get everything in clean, cold water, and then start arranging.

Any favorite tricks for arrangements?

I sometimes like to pull the petal back, so it changes the form of the tulip (see page 54). Some varieties you can do that to more than others—some are more pliable. And experiment with vessels. You can go from a fingerbowl with a simple blossom (see page 52) to the tallest vase with the beautiful stems of French tulips (see page 59). Tulips will work in pretty much any vase. It would be a fun challenge, actually—select any tulip and a random vase and somehow make it work.

What are some common mistakes with tulip arrangements?

You really have to take a step back when you're arranging and think about whether the vase calls for two dozen flowers or only five. It's all strategy, and scale is so important. Too-small tulips in a too-big vase just looks wrong. When in doubt, add more tulips.

Tulips don't need to be bright or vivid to make a statement. For this delicately hued display, Kevin combined silky 'White Parrot' and 'Salmon Parrot' tulips, green snowball viburnums, large single-petaled peonies, and the velvety foliage of scented geraniums. Spilling over the rim of an antique Sheffield silver wine cooler, the tulips function as the base of the arrangement. "Peonies can get buried, whereas tulips are great foundation flowers," says Kevin, who started with their sturdy stems to build upon.

To capture the voluptuous abundance of the season, double and single tulips—the more the better—are arranged in an early-twentieth-century glass pitcher that shows off the sturdy stems of 'Bronze Gem', 'Mrs. J. T. Scheepers', 'Fondante', 'Montreux', and 'Blushing Beauty' varieties. Alongside is a different category of the flower: smaller-scale botanical tulips (with their own foliage). In this Georgian blown-glass rummer (an eighteenth-century drinking glass), the comparison invites an appreciation of both.

OPPOSITE: This slender Juliska glass vase is the perfect container for long-stemmed single tulips. Cut the stems as long as the vase and line them up as straight as possible. Use a clear rubber band to secure bundles of clean stems, and stick to a limited variety—such as these two French tulips that complement each other in form and color.

ABOVE: When arranging flowers in an interesting container, don't miss the opportunity to call attention to it. Kevin arranged these yellow 'Monte Carlo' and bicolor 'Helmar' tulips in a shallow copper baking pan, to show off the sleek handles and blur the line between container and surroundings. "Think about the texture and material not only of the vessel, but of the surface," he advises. "An arrangement may be sitting on a highly polished metal, a mirrored tile, or a platform— why not have the flowers interact with the surface itself?"

OPPOSITE: 'Boston' variegated tulips, with their deep, rosy purple petals and yellow "throat" centers, serve as the inspiration for this beautiful spring bouquet's color palette. Joined with buttery narcissus, trout lilies, and deep violet lilacs— a departure from predictable pastels— the arrangement becomes a celebration of spring in unexpected colors. Always condition daffodil stems (see page 35) before mixing them with other cut flowers.

Rhododendron & Azalea

RHODODENDRON

OF ALL THE SHRUBS THAT FLOWER IN SPRING, RHODODENDRONS—ESPECIALLY THE AZALEAS—PROVIDE SOME OF THE MOST BRILLIANT DISPLAYS. I HAVE THEM PLANTED TOGETHER WITH TREE PEONIES IN A GARDEN JUST OUTSIDE MY SUMMER HOUSE, AND WHEN THEY BLOOM THIS TIME OF YEAR, THEY MAKE ONE CORNER OF MY FARM ERUPT WITH SPECTACULAR COLOR.

Azaleas can thrive in a wide variety of growing conditions, which makes them useful in many different landscapes. They are popularly referred to as the "royalty of the garden"—long adored for their brightly colored flowers and semi-evergreen foliage. Plant enthusiasts have selectively bred azaleas for years, producing thousands of different cultivars. My azalea collection is in a lightly wooded area near my blooming tree peonies, where they get filtered sunlight through the day—something they both prefer.

Azaleas are flowering shrubs in the Ericaceae family, which includes blueberries and mountain laurel, and are members of the genus *Rhododendron*. Some varieties can bloom as early as March, but most bloom in April or May, with blossoms lasting several weeks. The plants can survive for many years, and they continue to flower their entire lives.

*"I HAD NEVER CONSIDERED
RHODODENDRONS OR AZALEAS
IMPORTANT AS CUT FLOWERS
UNTIL I STARTED TO EXPERIMENT
WITH THEM IN SPRINGTIME
ARRANGEMENTS."*

Right nearby Skylands, in Maine, is the Asticou Azalea Garden. The garden, part of the Asticou Inn, was designed and built in 1956 by the owner, Charles K. Savage. In 1955, Beatrix Farrand, the renowned gardener and landscape architect, announced her plans to dismantle her fabulous gardens at her Reef Point estate in Bar Harbor. With the financial help of John D. Rockefeller, Jr., Savage was able to acquire many of those botanical specimens and fulfill his dream of building Asticou Azalea Garden, modeled after a classic Japanese design. In early spring, the garden begins with a flourish of cherry blossoms followed by a colorful explosion of azaleas in every imaginable shade. The garden is owned and maintained by Mount Desert Land and Garden Preserve and a committee of volunteers. One year not too long ago, after a stroll through Asticou with my own gardener from Katonah, we got many good ideas for what to plant around the pond on the farm, most notably the beautiful azaleas.

I had never considered rhododendrons or azaleas important as cut flowers until I started to experiment with them in springtime arrangements. Mixed with other seasonal perennials and bulbs, these amazing woody-stemmed flowers gave structure and shape to bouquets that could not be achieved with other flowers. Additionally, the florets are somewhat orchid-like in importance, and can also stand alone in small containers as a sort of specimen display that is colorful, interesting, and one of a kind.

At Turkey Hill, I had none of these cultivars, but at the farm on Bronson Road, in Fairfield, Connecticut, I did have an incredible fifty-year-old rhododendron hedge that measured more than 300 feet long and almost 20 feet high. It bloomed each spring for about three weeks—thousands of perfect clusters of mauvish rose flowers on shrubs covered in shiny elongated green leaves. Pruning a hedge like that did not detract from its glory, and I made giant arrangements for my home with just a few carefully chosen branches that arguably needed to be pruned, anyway!

I hated to leave that hedge; I miss it still. In East Hampton, where azalea and rhododendron grow profusely and thrive in the moist sea air, I have a similar though much smaller hedge, but it was not until I got my farm in Katonah that I started to study the culture of these spectacular shrubs in depth.

The garden around the Summer House in Katonah erupts in color every spring when a cluster of azaleas and tree peonies bursts into bloom. Azaleas can thrive in a wide variety of growing conditions, which makes them useful in many different landscapes.

GROWING
& ARRANGING

*ALL AZALEAS ARE RHODODENDRONS, BUT NOT ALL RHODODENDRONS
ARE AZALEAS. THE GENUS BOASTS HUNDREDS OF SPECIES AND
THOUSANDS OF HYBRIDS AND CULTIVARS IN AN ASTOUNDING VARIETY
OF COLORS, TEXTURES, SHAPES, AND SIZES—FROM TINY 2-INCH
AZALEA BLOSSOMS TO "BIG-LEAVED RHODIES" WITH 3-FOOT FOLIAGE.*

HOW TO GROW

The difference between azaleas and other rhododendrons is not strictly defined; generally, rhododendrons are evergreen and azaleas are deciduous or semi-evergreen (meaning they keep their leaves at the tips of their branches throughout the winter). The number of stamens is another indicator: Most azaleas have five, while other rhododendrons have at least ten. Azaleas and other rhododendrons have bloom times that range from early spring through midsummer, and their flowers come in almost every color of the rainbow. Azalea flowers are typically funnel-shaped, while other rhododendrons have bell-shaped blooms with thicker petals. All are quite easy to grow.

ZONE Some rhododendrons are more amenable than others to very cold winters or very hot summers, so it's important to choose one that is right for your zone. Some varieties are hardy to Zone 4 and others only to Zone 6. The tropical group known as Vireyas is hardy in Zones 10 and 11. Rhododendrons often have shallow roots and should be mulched well for winter; evergreen varieties benefit from winter protection in cold areas. The stems of azaleas, which are thinner than those of rhododendrons, can be brittle in cold weather, so they are best situated away from heavily trafficked areas.

SOIL Rhododendrons (including azaleas) flourish in acidic soil (pH 4.5 to 6). Soils in rainy areas tend to be acidic, while those in arid regions can be more alkaline. Avoid planting in soil near a house's foundation, as the cement may leach alkaline material. Test and amend with organic matter as needed (coffee grounds, finely milled pine bark, peat moss, or composted leaves are good choices); make sure your soil is not only acidic but also rich, moist, and well draining. Rhododendron roots can be relatively shallow; spread mulch to keep the roots cool and moist.

LIGHT Rhododendrons (including azaleas) prefer shady sites with a few hours of filtered light each day. Don't give them full sun, especially in warmer climates.

CHOOSING When selecting shrubs to plant, always examine the root systems. Make sure the roots are strong, with even branches and no signs of disease. With potted options, choose a plant that is not flowering. Like lilacs and other shrubs, the plant directs all its energy into flowering in order to fulfill its primary goal of reproduction; this leaves the unestablished root systems without proper nutrients. Healthy roots produce better plants. You should be able to pull the whole plant and root system out of the pot, without the roots breaking off—and without seeing endless

My dedicated azalea bed in Katonah contains several varieties to provide more visual interest. We sited the large bed in a shady, wooded area where the shrubs can get filtered sunlight throughout the day.

A single, massive rhododendron flower head sits at the bottom of a wide glass punch bowl. Kevin wanted to magnify the focus on the blossom and its dark throat: "It reminds me of Japanese fighting fish," he says. "I didn't fill the whole bowl with water, to keep the flower head resting below the rim of the glass." Kevin cut the stem all the way at the top and submerged the entire bottom of the flower in water. This is an arrangement that wouldn't be as effective from far away; let it have its close-up by putting it in the center of a dining table. *OPPOSITE:* Here, Kevin arranged rhododendron blossoms in a pair of Moroccan paintbrush holders. Their individual tubes allow for each short branch to reach water, and for the green leaves and containers to play off the red mophead blooms. "Anything on opposite sides of the color wheel, like red and green, will work well together in an arrangement," says Kevin. Again, cut the flower heads short, with their collar of leaves remaining intact. Place arrangements like these down the center length of a table or buffet.

circles of roots around the inside of the pot, a sign that it's been sitting too long. Look for medium-dark green leaves; avoid pale foliage.

PLANTING Plant in the spring about an inch below the surface. Apply a fertilizer for acid-loving plants along with a top dressing of high-quality organic mulch and compost. For the Katonah azaleas, we also use Azomite, which boosts the mineral content of the soil.

WATERING Keep the soil around rhododendrons (including azaleas) moist and spongy but well drained. Their root systems are quite shallow and can dry out easily, so remember to water a few times a week (or more frequently during hot spells).

PRUNING Because many rhododendrons flower on branches that are at least a year old, having set flower buds the summer before, it's best to prune your shrub right after it blooms, and only when needed (if, for example, you notice that the plant is beginning to crowd its neighbors). Think of it as deadheading taken to the next level. Rhododendron leaves erupt in a rosette around the stem; to prune, cut branches back to just above one of the whorls. Below each whorl are the dormant, slender leaf buds that will develop. Cut no more than 15 to 20 inches, and try not to shorten a branch by more than half. If you've inherited a truly ungainly plant, it may take a few seasons (or years) to finish the pruning process without inflicting too much damage. At the farm, we tend to cut off only dead or broken branches—rhododendrons have an elegant natural habit (the term for the growing shape of the plant) that is best left alone.

As for azaleas, paying attention to nodes is unnecessary for many of them; there are so many latent buds that the branch will flower no matter what. Azaleas can become bare in the middle, with leaves only at the tips. To help your shrub regain fullness, thin outer branches in order to expose smaller inner ones; the additional sunlight they receive will encourage them to fill in. Or cut off just a couple of inches every year (this is called tipping back), which stunts some growth at the end of the branch, keeping the plant full rather than letting it spread out.

TROUBLESHOOTING If your azalea plant is diseased, has suffered winter cold damage, or is simply aged and ungainly and requires a total overhaul, try a rejuvenation: In late winter or early spring, before new growth starts, cut all stems to about 8 inches above the ground. (Don't try this with larger rhododendrons, including *Rhododendron fortunei* and *R. arboreum,* or many hybrids and smooth-barked varieties; none will respond well when cut way down.) Before a rejuvenation, prepare the plant by fertilizing and mulching it in the spring, to promote vigorous root growth. Fertilize again after growth resumes in the spring following the rejuvenation, and water during any dry spells that summer. You may lose a year or two of great azalea blooms, but in the end your plant will grow back healthier and fuller.

Rhododendrons (including azaleas) can be susceptible to a fungal condition called root rot, caused by a mold in the soil, especially when newly transplanted. If you notice off-color, drooping foliage or discolored, dying roots, cut the branches 6 to 8 inches beyond the diseased portion, sterilize your tools with a solution of alcohol or water and bleach, and use fungicide to protect neighboring plants. Don't water diseased plants from overhead, and make sure the soil is very well drained to prevent the disease.

Keep in mind that rhododendron plants can be toxic to dogs. Consider your dog's personality when planning a garden—some animals love to chew on plants and trees, while others aren't interested. If your pet is a fan of eating greenery and is allowed to roam free in your yard, be sure to fence off any dangerous plants.

HOW TO ARRANGE

CUTTING Rhododendrons (including azaleas) are not commonly thought of as arrangement flowers; they are most often viewed from afar and never taken off the bush. But as beautiful as they appear en masse in the garden, their blossoms can be just as spectacular when viewed close-up. With most rhododendrons, cut just the flower, leaving a short stem for water intake. They have woody branches, a structure that doesn't lend itself to cutting long stems. Use secateurs or a sharp knife to split the ends about 1 to 2 inches vertically, so the plant can take in more water, and use in low arrangements.

MAINTAINING The blossoms can be long-lived once cut. Rhododendron foliage, with its leathery green leaves, can also be beautiful, and well suited in arrangements, as it holds up for an equal length of time. Azaleas have smaller, wispier foliage, which isn't mature when the shrub blossoms—you'll see flowers first, and later the leaves.

ARRANGING "I always thought of rhododendrons and azaleas as filler flowers, but they're at their best when they're the center of attention," Kevin says. "Their stamens have a really pretty character. They curl upward, and can add a little spark and fizz to denser arrangements of flowers like peonies." Rhododendrons are often top-heavy, so choose a vessel with sides that can secure the flower. Azaleas are more stable and can nestle into taller vessels. Despite how full and dense an azalea shrub can look from afar, the individual branches can be fairly sparse; their smaller flowers mix well with other blooms, such as tulips or peonies. The biggest step is simply remembering to bring these blossoms inside. Cut a rhododendron short and put it in a glass, or embrace the idea of small flowers in multiples when you have a big bunch of azaleas (as shown on page 63).

Cut rhododendron flower heads are arranged in a collection of small glasses, set on tiered American pressed-glass cake stands for an epergne effect. (French epergnes were tiered bowls or trays traditionally made of silver, but glass came into use at the beginning of the twentieth century.) Kevin mimicked the effect with a drinking glass at the top and short glasses all around.

Lilacs look beautiful arranged by the armload with leaves as sole accompaniment. "I really like it when I can get the lilac foliage to live, but if I can't do that, I like to use other types of foliage, especially smoke bush leaves," Kevin says. In a French Art Deco painted cast-iron trumpet vase, he paired 'Angel White' and 'Beauty of Moscow' lilacs with smoke bush leaves, whose plum-brown shade perfectly complements the lilac's pale lavender. "Foliage can really help to achieve the overall shape you're aiming for, especially when the flowers don't necessarily cooperate."

Lilac

SYRINGA

MANY YEARS AGO I READ A CHARMING BOOK TITLED ELIZABETH AND HER GERMAN GARDEN, PUBLISHED IN 1898. IT WAS A MEMOIR BY ELIZABETH VON ARNIM, AN ENGLISHWOMAN WHO IN THE LATTER PART OF THE NINETEENTH CENTURY MOVED WITH HER HUSBAND TO HIS FAMILY'S LANDS IN POTSDAM, GERMANY. THE BOOK AND ITS DESCRIPTIONS OF HER ASTONISHING GARDENS REKINDLED MEMORIES OF THE GARDENS I DREAMED ABOUT WHILE GROWING UP.

It was as if Elizabeth and I had had the same dreams as children—those of light and air and vast expanses of romantic plantings, intoxicatingly scented and delicately colored. Elizabeth had a lilac hill that seemed to stretch endlessly through space. The lilacs that grew around and near my childhood house were most certainly the old-fashioned *Syringa vulgaris*. Beautifully colored and perfumed, they were common in our neighborhood but very special to me. One of my favorite Greek myths was the story of the god Pan who pursued the nymph Syrinx and turned her into a hollow reed from which he fashioned his first flute, or "panpipe." An early name for the lilac was pipe tree or blow stem. This

*"SOME OF MY LILAC SHRUBS ARE
ACTUALLY BUSHY TREES, 15 FEET OR
SO IN HEIGHT, AND THE LILACS
RANGE IN COLOR FROM WHITE TO
DEEPEST PURPLE-BLACK."*

identification of the tree with a musical instrument and a legend was what growing up for me was all about: literature and gardening and learning and experiencing.

I married in 1961, and on our car trips throughout the Northeast I tried to schedule visits for the time of year when lilacs would be in bloom. The Arnold Arboretum in Massachusetts was a treasure trove of older varieties. The area in and around Rochester's Highland Park neighborhood, designed by Frederick Law Olmsted, is filled with vast numbers of the shrubs in spectacular colors. When I lived in Manhattan, I would visit my sister-in-law in Bedford, New York, during lilac time to pick to my heart's content. It was then that I vowed to always have great numbers of these productive and dependable shrubs growing wherever I lived. When, as a young couple, we purchased our home in Westport, Connecticut, I was thrilled by the large clumps of lilac shrubs that seemed to be growing everywhere. You can imagine my utter dismay when in spring the leaves grew no larger than a privet's leaves. Indeed that is what all the shrubs were—very overgrown privets. It took several years before the tiny hybrid shrubs I ordered from catalogs matured to flower-bearing size. Many years later, there were plenty of fragrant flowers at Turkey Hill in May and June.

And every year, I added to my collection. When I moved to Katonah, I found myself back at square one as far as lilacs were concerned. There was not one of these outstanding shrubs on the 150 acres. So I collected and planted a sizable assortment in two long matching borders the length of the entire Maple Avenue house. Within three years, the display was very showy, and the numbers of blooms so exciting. Now some of the shrubs are actually bushy trees, 15 feet or so in height, and the lilacs range in color from white to deepest purple-black.

At Skylands, I planted one area of the vegetable garden with lilac shrubs I found at Surry Gardens in Surry, Maine. I planted them the second year I owned the house, and now, more than fifteen years later, I have an unusual and gorgeous array of well-flowering shrubs. How wonderful to anticipate need and desire, and then to fulfill both with the most amazing plants.

There are more than four hundred varieties of *Syringa vulgaris* alone, in a range of colors, fragrances, and sizes. We grow many of them at the farm in Katonah, such as the bicolor 'Sensation' pictured here. Their cold-hardiness makes them a natural in Maine as well, where we harvest armloads of lilacs every spring.

LILAC 75

GROWING
& ARRANGING

*THE COMMON LILAC (SYRINGA) HAS BEEN A BELOVED
PART OF THE AMERICAN LANDSCAPE FOR CENTURIES; THE FLOWERS
ARE SWEETLY FRAGRANT AND COLORFUL. WHEN GIVEN PLENTY
OF SUN AND WELL-DRAINED SOIL, THEY ARE INCREDIBLY STURDY AND
UNDEMANDING—AND BOUND TO THRIVE AND DELIGHT.*

HOW TO GROW

Lilacs thrive in their native climate of somewhat chilly, mountainous regions. Though heat can be their undoing, nurseries have bred hybrids that can handle warmer zones—even in the dry heat of Texas. The *Syringa* x *laciniata*, with its elegant, fine-textured foliage, can also fare well in warmer areas, even after its pale-lavender flowers have faded.

ZONE Lilac shrubs grow in cooler climates with chilling periods, Zones 4 to 7, and bloom for just two weeks in late spring and early summer. In order to flower, it's essential for common lilacs to experience a proper winter chill. Without one, they struggle and bloom irregularly; some don't flower at all. If you live in a location that has mild winters (Zones 7 and 8), choose a Descanso hybrid (specifically bred for "no-chill" climates); some cultivars, such as 'Blue Skies', 'Excel', and 'Sister Justina', have been bred for even warmer regions (Zones 8 and 9).

SOIL Lilacs need well-drained soil that is rich in organic matter and fairly neutral in pH—slightly acidic or alkaline levels are fine. New England soils, including the soil on the farm at Katonah, are often very acidic and require some amendments to ensure proper lilac growth. We treat that soil with composted horse manure, superphosphate, and Azomite, a finely ground natural trace mineral powder made from sea bed clay that functions as both a fertilizer and soil remineralizer.

Lilacs need good drainage in order to thrive, so it's crucial to check your soil before planting. It should retain enough moisture to thoroughly nourish the root system, but drain quickly. To test, dig a hole about 1 foot deep and 8 inches in diameter. Fill with water, and then check back in an hour. If the water has not drained, choose another site.

LIGHT In order to flourish, common lilacs need lots of sunshine, at least six to eight hours daily, ideally in the morning (when it's not as hot). Lilacs grown in partial sun or shade will not flower well, and even a shrub planted in full sun years ago may now find itself shaded by larger trees that have grown around it. In this case, start with a new plant in a sunnier location.

CHOOSING Lilacs can be purchased in bare-root form, as a potted root-ball, or as a partially grown bush. Bare roots are dormant plants often sold or shipped in bags of moist sawdust or wood shavings, with a few bare twigs extending from the root clump. Bare-root stems should be about the thickness of a finger; avoid anything thin or brittle. Make sure the roots are intact and that the stems are fully dormant—they should be somewhat flexible and will reveal some green underneath if scratched with a fingernail. When

Lilacs, such as Katonah's 'Firmament', bloom for only about two weeks in spring, but the plants themselves—which can grow up to 15 feet tall—can live a very long time. Some have survived more than a century. That longevity requires tender loving care, of course, including a good amount of sun and water, and regular pruning in late spring and early summer, just after the blooms have finished.

When the lilacs are in full bloom in Katonah, the air is filled with their sweet scent. Because of my lifelong love of lilacs, I grow many, many varieties, and when they're ready to be cut, we need more than a wicker flower basket to gather them for arrangements. Some of the varieties include 'Wedgwood Blue', 'President Poincare', 'Little Boy Blue', 'Atheline Wilbur', 'Paul Thirion', 'Sensation', 'Angel White', and 'Adelaide Dunbar'. After carefully cutting them, we fill up the bed of the Kawasaki Mule to transport them through the linden allée and back to the house for prepping and arranging.

selecting a potted bush or root-ball, carefully examine the root system to ensure it is healthy, and choose a plant with strong, even branches and no signs of disease. There should be no flowers on the plant; this indicates the plant is funneling all its energy into flower production rather than establishing a strong root system. If you remove the plant from the pot, the root-ball should come out intact; but if there are so many roots that they are circling the pot or growing out of the bottom, the plant has been potted for too long. Choose another.

PLANTING Early spring and fall are the best times to plant; many growers prefer to plant lilacs in fall, especially in milder climates. Dig a large hole that is two to three times as wide as the root-ball, and place the top of the root-ball level with the surface of the hole. If planting a bare root, the top layer of roots should sit a few inches below the surface. Fill in with soil and water thoroughly to stabilize the plant and guard against air pockets under the surface. In addition to selecting a spot that is large enough to accommodate the mature size of your lilac plant, choose one that has good air circulation to reduce the likelihood of developing fungal diseases such as powdery mildew.

Don't expect blooms the first year—or even the second—and if any develop, cut them off to help the plant focus its energy into creating a strong root system (see Pruning, right). From the third year onward, blooming should be prolific. The common lilac is often considered the best-smelling variety and boasts the largest flowers, but its bloom time is short. Include other lilac species to double your blooming time—and you'll sometimes see a bonus of repeat flowerings around Labor Day, as well.

WATERING Water young plants regularly at planting, during bloom, and in heavy growth periods. Once established, lilacs are fairly drought-tolerant. Aim for an inch of water per week, supplemented by you if your area doesn't get enough rain, and water more frequently during bloom season—an inch twice a week instead of once, depending on your soil type and how the plant looks. After blooming ends, gradually cut back on watering, unless your area is experiencing unnaturally hot or dry weather.

FERTILIZING Fertilize lilacs early in the season with a balanced organic fertilizer. After pruning, use compost, composted manure, or a balanced chemical fertilizer, and ensure that the soil pH is close to neutral. These amendments and some good mulch will help to stimulate vigorous new growth and better flowering in years to come.

PRUNING Mature lilacs need pruning to promote flowering, to reshape, and to remove unwanted suckers (shoots that develop where the stem meets the ground; see Propagating, below). Don't be shy with your clippers; lilacs are hardy and can withstand a lot of cutting, but timing is crucial. Almost immediately after blooming, the shrub begins to set buds for next season's show. You should prune right after the blooms have faded, and never after the first week of July, or you risk losing future blossoms. To prune properly, cut any diseased, misshapen, and unproductive stems at or just below soil level. Remove the large, unattractive seedpods that form after flowers fade, and prune out any dead, damaged, or diseased branches as you see them, cutting just above a bud. Remove old, woody stems to encourage air circulation and increase exposure to sunlight; proper, yearly pruning can ensure reliable blooming for more than a decade. 'Palibin Meyer' (*Syringa meyeri*) and 'Miss Kim Manchurian' lilacs (*Syringa pubescens* ssp. *patula*), both of which we grow at Katonah, can be relatively small shrubs (under 8 feet) with a twiggy habit. Little pruning other than deadheading is required on these types.

PROPAGATING Lilacs are typically clump-forming, producing new shoots, or suckers, from the base of the trunk. Suckers can be unsightly and drain the shrub's strength, so cut them off in order to funnel energy to the mother plant. Suckers can also be used to propagate new shrubs. Simply remove soil from the top of the roots, cut off suckers with pruning shears, and then replace the soil. Larger suckers can be dug up with their roots intact and grown in pots until they are large enough to be transplanted.

Freshly cut lilacs create a study in variegated shades within the grove at Katonah. We've left 10 to 12 inches of stem in order to adjust the height as we arrange the flowers. Normally the lilacs would be put in a bucket of water immediately after cutting. On this morning, however, Kevin was working very quickly to gather as many blooms as possible for an event, so he cut them and tossed them into the center to be gathered into water-filled buckets in the Kawasaki for transport.

TROUBLESHOOTING If a lilac shrub doesn't flower regularly, it could be due to lack of sun, poorly timed pruning, or your climate. Make sure to choose a variety suitable for your region's hardiness zone. The most prevalent lilac problems are powdery mildew fungus, lilac borer, and scale (both oyster-shell scale and prunicola scale are common). Some lilac issues affect certain regions more than others—the foggy chill of San Francisco makes mildew more of a risk, while warmer regions of the South attract more insects, including aphids and scale. Powdery mildew appears in the form of white patches dusting the leaves, and, though unattractive, it is rarely serious. Borers leave ⅛-inch holes in stems and larger branches, often 1 to 2 feet above ground level. A minor infestation might be ignored, but a plant with more than a few borers should be attended to by a professional. Oyster-shell scale is aptly named, as the pests look like tiny oyster shells covering the stems, while prunicola scale covers bark with a dusty white mass. Control scale by pruning heavily infested branches; remove young "crawlers" with a hard spray of water from a garden hose. My lilacs are generally pest-free, so we rarely need to spray, but dormant oil would be my first choice if the need arose. Also known as summer oil, it's a type of horticultural oil used to kill pests by smothering them. It is especially effective on aphids, scale, and mites. It was once only used during the dormant season, as the oil could burn foliage under the heat of the summer sun; new formulations are much lighter and most can be used year-round.

HOW TO ARRANGE

CUTTING Cut lilacs right at their peak, when color and scent are strongest, or when the flowers on the cluster are one-quarter to one-half open, depending on your preference. Leave 10 to 12 inches of stem so you'll be able to cut the lilacs down to desired heights when arranging. Be sure to put them in water immediately to preserve the blooms (if you're picking from the garden, take a bucket of water with you). Kevin puts freshly cut lilacs in very hot water—as hot as he can get it from the tap. Hot water helps to soften the woody lilac stem and allow it to take up more water. After this initial treatment, arrange in cold water to help prevent wilting. To prep the woody branches, use your pruners to split the stem a couple of inches up the center, crosshatch with secateurs by clipping an X into the end, or crush the last few inches with a hammer or rubber mallet to help them draw more water.

MAINTAINING Lilacs are sometimes thought of as notoriously short-lived cut flowers, but the common variety can last a week or more as long as the plant is healthy. Keep arrangements out of direct light, and refresh the water every day or two. (The water will get dirty quickly, so keep an eye on it.) If you're not able to keep up with the water replacement, as with a very large arrangement in a heavy container, at least choose a vessel that will conceal the water and stems.

ARRANGING Lilacs are excellent arrangement flowers, though not everyone thinks to take them off the bush and bring them into the home. When arranging, always use stems with vigorous foliage and fresh blooms. Strip any leaves that would sit below the waterline, but don't discard the foliage entirely. Try retaining the leaves on the shortest stems, so that they form a bottom border of green around the lip of the vessel.

Kevin and I like to gather lilacs in two or more hues (for example, a light lavender and a dark purple) and group them by color within a vase. In a large vessel, a huge, billowing cloud of lilacs is beautiful to look at, and makes for a strikingly bold statement as a centerpiece—yet the flowers themselves are so delicate that the overall impression is of softness. To construct a large-scale arrangement like the one on pages 88–89, Kevin built an architectural foundation within the planter by using the long lilac stems themselves. The first few branches were placed almost horizontally and carefully weaved together to form a lattice as the arrangement grew. Then the remaining branches and foliage were able to nestle into the remaining spaces, building upon each other. In this way, the flowers form their own structure and support system. You can try this technique with a smaller vessel by creating a grid of tape across the top of the vase (see page 262).

KEVIN SHARKEY

One of the great things about lilacs is that they have all these variations in so many colors, and they somehow all flatter and challenge each other equally in arrangements.

What are your favorite varieties?

Lilacs are one of the flowers I grew up around, so I have such a personal reference to them. There was a woman who lived down the street from us who had these deep purple, almost black lilacs—the blackest I had ever seen. It was all I could do not to steal those lilacs. Then throughout high school, I worked for the Arnold Arboretum in Boston—they are known for their lilacs—and it was there I discovered that true Wedgwood blue color; it's just beautiful. The ones at Martha's farm in Katonah have become my favorites.

What do you like to pair in arrangements with lilacs?

I like lilacs best on their own. But when you mix them with tulips and peonies—although it doesn't seem as contemporary—you might think it would look vulgar, but it's actually quite beautiful. I also love using certain foliage with lilacs, such as horse chestnut or privet leaves, and, if sturdy enough, the lilacs' own foliage (see opposite). In early spring, many plant leaves are too fragile and won't hold up after being cut—lilac foliage included. But when you can find something hardier, like raspberry leaves, the texture and color of a green leaf is an excellent complement to the blossoms.

How do you decide on a vase?

Height and texture come into play a lot. Most of the vases that I use with lilacs are on the large side, and I tend to pick vases that are opaque, to hide the branches. I like trumpet shapes, ginger jars, or cylinders because I like to let the stems and flower heads spread out.

When shopping for lilacs, what should you look for?

I would make sure the blooms are not all fully blown—you want some buds so you know the stem is healthy and so that they can open in the vase. Although I usually like long stems, I think shorter is better if you are buying cut flowers from a store, because they have a better chance of getting water to the blossom (and of course crushing or notching the stem is key, see Cutting, page 83). Hydration is especially important if they've been deprived of it while on display at the shop.

What are some common mistakes when arranging lilacs?

I think people sometimes miss the opportunity to celebrate the flower itself. Just keep it simple, and remember to use multiples. Lilacs aren't meant to be treated too strictly or too quietly.

How do you make cut lilacs last longer?

Lilacs are not necessarily short-lived flowers. If they are cut from a healthy plant, they can last a full week or even longer. Generally when the flowers are from a garden, you know how fresh they are, and they are worth the cutting. When they're from a flower market, it can get dicey. The variety can make a difference, too—I find that the common lilac lasts the longest in a vase. The more elaborate varieties, in my experience, can be more delicate—and white lilacs seem to be more susceptible to quickly wilting. Take care with the leaves—the branch structure of a lilac can be complicated and you will have to spend a lot of time removing the leaves and cleaning up the stem. If you have plenty of clean, fresh water, you don't need flower food or chemicals to keep the arrangement looking great.

To add motion and a theatrical touch to an arrangement, Kevin mixed lilacs of deep purple with white, lavender, and bluish lavender; then, to draw the eye down from the frothy main event, he added lavender wisteria and let it trail onto the table in Martha's servery. A flowering vine like wisteria is a bit unexpected for a flower arrangement, but the way that it cascades in a steep vertical from the cast-iron vase really captivates the eye.

When it comes to flowers, sometimes there is no such thing as "enough." One of those times is lilac season. Take advantage of the abundance and mass the flowers in a sculptural bouquet. Using a cage-form flower frog lets some blooms (here, 'Firmament' and 'Wedgwood Blue') remain upright while others drape over the edges of this French cast-iron vase.

OPPOSITE: Combining the voluptuous blooms of the lilac with smaller, more delicate flowers and shapely foliage can produce a stunning arrangement. Here, Kevin mixed clouds of cream-colored 'Angel White' lilacs with the nodding white flowers of bleeding heart (*Dicentra*), sky-blue forget-me-nots (*Myosotis sylvatica*), and Persian lily (*Fritillaria persica*) for the subtlest hints of color. The glass vase, purchased on a trip to Australia, is comprised of fused cylinders, giving each flower breathing room.

PREVIOUS PAGES:
This big, bold arrangement for the living room at Skylands offers a stunning centerpiece for the table. Several shades of lilac are combined, some in full bloom and others in bud, which adds texture to the display. A lattice-like weave of branches holds the lilacs together (see Arranging, page 83) so that the individual stems stay in place and build height. "Very few flowers can go from a painted wrought-iron trumpet to a gold china vase to clear glass, ceramic, or even, as here, cement," says Kevin. "It just goes to show you how versatile lilacs can be in terms of playing with other materials." Don't shy away from lilacs at a dinner party: "There are a lot of flowers that have such a heavy aroma that you wouldn't want to eat with them nearby," says Kevin. "But lilacs, although they have a fragrance, are certainly welcome at the table."

ABOVE: Just as masses of lilacs can perform in a large arrangement, a solitary bloom or a few stems work beautifully in small vessels, such as a pair of gold vermeil vases (a Mother's Day gift from Kevin). "The blossoms are particularly compatible with vessels that have a strong visual point of view, like gold." A matching set makes a dynamic duo, as an alternative to a larger, singular display. 'Sensation' lilacs are studded with airy green hellebore, placed one at a time into the spaces left by the lilac stems.

A large and shapely *Astilboides tabularis* leaf can make a big statement, adding asymmetry and dimension to this arrangement dominated by 'Adelaide Dunbar' lilac florets. Placing the earthenware pot on a pedestal of wood adds another layer of visual impact. Try positioning a vase on a decorative plate or tray to boost the scale of your arrangement.

Alliums, or ornamental onions, are one of nature's eccentric beauties. They can stand on their own as the stars of an arrangement. This tall, dark, and slender contemporary studio-ceramic vase gives white 'Mount Everest', which can climb up to 4 feet tall, even more dramatic presence. Kevin staggered the heights of the stems to give this arrangement a freeform look and to keep the blooms from canceling each other out. Foliage (these are *Rodgersia aesculifolia* leaves) softens the bouquet and draws the eye to areas that would otherwise be left bare.

Allium

ALLIUM

THERE IS NOTHING QUITE LIKE A 'GLOBEMASTER',
CHRISTOPHII, *OR* GIGANTEUM *ALLIUM IN BLOOM.*
THEY ARE TALL AND IMPOSING, BURSTING WITH HUGE
BALLS OF PURPLE. THEY PEAK DURING THE TIME IN THE
GARDEN WHEN TULIPS HAVE FADED AND THE BIG
SHOWY PERENNIALS HAVE NOT YET COME INTO BLOOM.

The plants are not liked by deer and rabbits, take up very little room at ground level, and can be packed into tight spaces. Most important, planted among catmint, poppies, and comfrey, as in my long pergola garden, the varying shades and heights and textures of the allium create a veritable showstopping event.

Nonetheless, alliums pose a challenge for the home gardener. They bloom once a year on stiff upright stems and, unless planted in larger numbers, can look out of place in a border. If they emerge before the last frost, their leaves might turn brown and look in poor health during the blooming period. They do not multiply like daffodils and countless other small bulbs. They may last just one season. And because they are, actually, onions, they can smell like onions when blooming.

I started planting allium, all different types, in my Turkey Hill garden. I loved the

accents of purple and mauve and violet, gently protruding over the other plants. I especially favor the very large round blooming types that are made up of hundreds of purplish florets on tall stems, including 'Ambassador', 'Firmament', *A. giganteum*, 'Globemaster', and 'Mars'.

My favorite of all is what I have nicknamed "fireworks"—*A. schubertii*, producing on each stem a volleyball-sized bloom with rosy, purple star-shaped florets. I plant these incredible bulbs at the front of the pergola in Katonah and in the long borders and beneath hostas in the terrace beds at Skylands. In Maine, they bloom right around the Fourth of July and they are indeed a cause for celebration.

If you are adventurous, there are other types you should try in your garden: *A. stipitatum* 'White Giant', similar to *A. giganteum* and 'Mount Everest'; *A. unifolium*, a shorter version with half-dollar-sized umbels in pink, lavender, or white; *A. karataviense*, which has broad glaucous leaves and comes in bright pink-red or lilac; and *A. bulgaricum*, with pendant greenish-white flowers tinged with purple.

For the vegetable gardener, try *A. senescens*, an ornamental onion; *A. altaicum*, another ornamental onion, which is architectural in form and very pretty in an arid garden; and, of course, *A. tuberosum*, or garlic chives, which have not only lovely white flowers but also delicious leaves that can be tied into knots, and steamed or sautéed in the Chinese style. The latter are truly perennial and last in the garden for many years.

There is one story I tell everyone when the subject of alliums comes up, the gist of which is "never, ever, tell children to 'just look, don't touch' when it comes to alliums." The attraction is just too great, and the ball-shaped flowers snap off easily, and can be played with for hours. It's much better to tell them, "No! No! No!" Forbid them to even go near them! If not, every flower will be pulled off, played with, and your garden will be sad without its beautiful umbels of purple and blue and pink and white. Trust me! I've seen it happen many times. And who can blame the children? These beautiful, exuberant puffballs are nothing short of irresistible.

Alliums' sturdy stems make them particularly suited to upright arrangements. To create a looser-looking ensemble, Kevin crossed the stems to make a framework for a gathering of rose-purple *A. schubertii* (at left) and 'Purple Sensation' and white *Allium nigrum* (at right) in vintage blown-glass leech bowls. (I have a collection of these curious vessels, which doctors once used to store the worms used in the practice of bloodletting.) Allium flowers fade beautifully from one shade to another throughout their bloom cycle.

GROWING
& ARRANGING

*ALLIUMS ARE POPULAR, AND WITH GOOD REASON:
THE UNUSUAL, SPHERICAL, STARRY FLOWERS ON LONG,
SKINNY STEMS CAN ADD STRIKING BURSTS OF
COLOR AND TEXTURE TO ANY GARDEN OR ARRANGEMENT.*

HOW TO GROW

Spring- and summer-blooming alliums have many attractive features, including that they're adored by pollinators like bees and butterflies, yet resistant to rabbits, rodents, and deer.

ZONE Alliums come from the United States, Central Asia, the Middle East, and China, among other places. Very few exist in the Southern Hemisphere, however, so although some species and cultivars do well when grown from Zones 3 to 9, on the whole they do not perform well south of Zone 8. Check each species' growing details carefully.

SOIL To get alliums to thrive, you need to plant them in soil that is loaded with compost and other organic matter, and make sure that it is well drained to avoid bulb rot. From early spring until the alliums have finished blooming, feed them with a slow-release bulb-specific fertilizer containing bone meal, potassium, and superphosphate, such as Holland Bulb Booster (9:9:6).

LIGHT Grow these showy bulbs in a garden that gets full sun, even in the height of summer, when surrounding trees are leafed out. You may have luck with some shade, however; I've lined the length of my pergola in Katonah with alliums and planted others in the flower garden and around the houses; some have grown nicely in partial shade.

CHOOSING Bulbs vary in size but all should be firm. Ensure that the bulbs are fresh and keep them dry until planting, as they are very prone to black mildew.

PLANTING The time to plant allium bulbs is in autumn, before the ground has frozen. Plant them at a depth of about three times the diameter of the bulb, with the somewhat flattened root end facing downward. Spacing depends on the species (from the large *A. giganteum* at 12 inches apart to the more petite *A. caeruleum* at 2 inches apart). Alliums (especially the smaller-flowered varieties) can return year after year under the right conditions. The larger-flowered varieties tend to die out after three to four years, however, so you'll need to replace them with new bulbs.

WATERING While the plants are growing, give them at least half an inch of water every week from early spring through the end of bloom. The dormant plants like dry soil, so don't water them after they've finished blooming. However, if other, thirstier plants share the same bed, be sure to give them the water they need—they'll soak up the moisture before it compromises the alliums.

PRUNING Don't remove the leaves, no matter how unsightly, until they have completely browned. They're needed to supply energy to the bulbs. You can remove the spent flowers

Alliums create fireworks wherever they turn up. I grow many varieties, and like to combine several in a single bouquet. Kevin gathered 'Mount Everest', 'Globemaster', 'Gladiator', and other alliums at the potting shed at Turkey Hill. He arranged them in a vintage European glazed bread bowl as well as in American galvanized tin pails. The groups show off the alliums' range in size, shape, and color—the deep purples, lavenders, silver, and white all work together. It's as if he captured shooting stars in motion. One of my favorite varieties is the spiky, sunburst-shaped *A. schubertii*, displayed all by itself in the low tin bucket.

before they go to seed, then save the seeds and propagate from them, or divide the bulbs. I love the look of the dry flowers in the fall, so we'll often leave them in the garden until they begin to deteriorate.

TROUBLESHOOTING One of the few downsides to growing alliums is that, like many bulbous plants, they have leaves that can turn scraggly when their flowers bloom—one reason why many gardeners interplant alliums with perennials. The latter cover the limp foliage at alliums' bases without obstructing the blooms up top. We use peonies, baptisia, catnip, and lilies.

HOW TO ARRANGE

CUTTING Harvest alliums when they are just fully bloomed. It's important to cut them in the early morning, using a sharp knife. Ornamental alliums can give off an onion scent, especially when the stems are crushed. Cutting cleanly helps to minimize the aroma.

Immediately put them in fresh water, and change it regularly. Most alliums should last about two weeks.

ARRANGING Arrangements can be minimal and modern or lush and romantic, but they are always captivating, thanks to the plants' otherworldly blossoms. You can leave the stems long or cut them short—allium is equally declarative as a bloom in a shallow vessel as with stems standing tall. If you're arranging a mass of alliums, use a trumpet-shaped vase to prevent the blossoms from sticking together (larger-flowered varieties are especially prone to this). Trim the stems to slightly different lengths for a staggered effect. Some small species can resemble tassels or pom-poms and are great for softening a mixed arrangement. The larger globes can look dramatic all alone.

ABOVE: By cutting the stem very short, you can turn one allium into a centerpiece by placing it in a small vessel or by grouping individual spheres. Here, Kevin used *A. albopilosum*, 'Firmament', 'Purple Sensation', and a dried blossom in pressed-glass sugar bowls in the sawtooth pattern. *OPPOSITE:* There is so much movement in the bloom of an allium, especially in *A. schubertii*, at far right, which resembles a starburst. It seems fitting, then, to arrange the sparklers singly (including *A. albopilosum*) in gleaming English brass candleholders set on a decorative tole tray.

This Japanese ginger jar was given to me many years ago. Until then, I had never seen a yellow, peach, or mauve tree peony, but obviously the painter of the bowl had. Finally my tree peonies have matured and now provide blooms of almost the same colors. Here, the flowers (a mix of old-fashioned peonies and Itoh hybrids) are paired with *Heuchera*, a perennial that loves shade in the garden and has heart-shaped leaves in hues of green, yellow, rust, brown, purple, and nearly black.

Peony

PAEONIA

ONE OF THE FLOWERS I MOST LOOK FORWARD TO SEEING EACH SPRING IS THE PEONY. IN THE GARDEN AT MY FARM, I HAVE CONCENTRATED ON THE CULTURE OF HERBACEOUS PEONIES AS WELL AS TREE PEONIES. ALTHOUGH RELATED, HERBACEOUS PEONIES BLOOM ON SOFT STEMS, WHICH DIE BACK TO THE GROUND EACH AUTUMN AND REEMERGE THE FOLLOWING YEAR.

Tree peonies bloom on woody branches much like those of trees. The form remains all year long, and it is important never to prune the tree peony unless removing dead wood. The most prized varieties of this type of peony are large, ornamental, tree-like shrubs that produce hundreds of blooms every year. With proper care and feeding, either type of peony should thrive and produce for many years in the garden.

Influenced by writers like Vita Sackville-West and Elizabeth von Arnim, both of whom grew lovely peonies, I was determined to have as many of these beautiful flowers as I could. For my first large peony garden, comprised of more than five hundred plants, I chose to stick to a pink palette, ranging from almost white to blush to pink to deeper rose. I conferred with my friend Roy Klehm, owner of Song Sparrow farm in Avalon,

It's easy to see why the Chinese called the herbaceous peony *sho yo*, "most beautiful." Here, morning dew clings to the leaves and intricately ruffled blooms of one of the many pink peonies at the farm in Katonah, a very full crown-form 'Madame de Verneville'. Early morning is the best time to cut peonies; gathering them in the cool of the day means they are much less likely to wilt.

Wisconsin. He directed me to varieties that would bloom over a period of about three to four weeks and would produce an abundance of gorgeous cut flowers. For years now, my friends and I have enjoyed a tremendous flower display each year in the large peony garden, and reveled in the beauty and proliferation of all those plants.

On my first trip to China in the 1970s, I visited Hangzhou, the capital of Zhejiang province, where the ancient Grand Canal waterway ends (it originates far away, in Beijing). The West Lake is the terminus, surrounded by gardens, pavilions, and arched bridges. It was there where I had my first glimpse of the amazing tree peonies that have grown in China for thousands of years. The shrubs were much taller than I and were blooming profusely. This flower is now the national flower of China, where it is known as *moutan*. About a thousand years ago tree peonies were transported to Japan, where gardeners took a great liking to this incredible flower, and they have hybridized many different types. The display of Japanese tree peonies in the Imperial Gardens is an incredible sight. Now, thanks to great suppliers, tree peonies are more readily available worldwide and even just a few of these plants make any garden extraordinary.

I have grown peonies in my Turkey Hill garden, in East Hampton, and now at the farm in Katonah. In 2011, Kevin and I created a story and video for the first digital edition of *Martha Stewart Living,* as well as for my daily show. I picked and Kevin arranged, and that was when the idea for this book came about. We made such a good team, and we collaborated very well—agreeing more often than not about how we should display the wonderful flowers, how we should enhance them with additional blooms and foliage—and we had a good deal of fun determining which containers were good for which flowers. I have also made an annual or semiannual peony party a tradition at the farm—it is special to see so many utterly beautiful plants blooming at the same time!

GROWING
& ARRANGING

PEONIES DON'T REQUIRE COMPLEX FERTILIZATION,
SPRAYING, PRUNING, OR DIVIDING, AND THEY CAN LIVE A
LONG, LONG TIME. WITH THEIR HARDY NATURES AND
BEAUTIFUL BLOOMS, IT'S NO WONDER BOTH HERBACEOUS AND
TREE PEONIES ARE A PERENNIAL GARDENER'S DREAM.

HOW TO GROW

Most peonies *(Paeonia)* are a cinch to grow once you understand their basic needs: at least six to eight hours of full summer sun and well-drained soil that's relatively free of competing plant roots. They don't take well to transplanting, so choose your location wisely. Peonies are deer resistant, making them very appealing to rural gardeners. A mature plant can produce more than one hundred flowers and each bloom can reach a size of 10 inches or more in diameter. Though the blooming season is short, peony plants offer handsome rich-green foliage that will stay vibrant in the garden until late fall, with some varieties turning a deep-red or copper color.

Peonies are generally divided into two groups: herbaceous peonies *(P. lactiflora)*, which are perennials that grow to about 3 feet tall and die back to the ground each winter, and slow-growing, woody-stemmed tree peonies *(P. suffruticosa)*, which can reach up to 6 feet at maturity (some can grow even taller with enough time and proper pruning). A third, newer group is that of intersectional peony hybrids (Itohs), which combine the traits of both, creating herbaceous plants with the flowers and foliage of a tree variety.

Tree peony cultivars have petals of shiny satin, while those from herbaceous peonies resemble a filmy silk. With their smaller stature, herbaceous peonies are especially versatile in a garden and, as one of the hardiest perennials, can easily outlive the gardeners who plant them. Though tree peonies remain slightly more expensive than their more popular herbaceous cousins, growing only one peony type is a missed opportunity for variety in your garden. Try planting plenty of herbaceous peonies to bloom in masses, but also plan for a few magnificent tree peonies. They can take three to four years after planting to come into full bloom—but when properly situated and planted, they are as close to immortal as any garden plant.

ZONE Native to dry, chilly mountainsides, most herbaceous peonies are hardy in Zones 2 to 7, but some varieties are suitable as far south as Zone 8. Tree peonies grow well in Zones 4 to 8, and some in Zone 9 on the Pacific coast. Though all peonies require winter chilling (four hundred hours of temperatures below 32 degrees) in order to flower, early bloomers, such as 'Abalone Pearl', are best in mild regions with hot summers because they open before the wilting heat. In regions with heavy summer rain, choose single forms and Japanese varieties, which don't collect water in their blossoms.

SOIL Peony shrubs prefer a neutral to slightly alkaline soil that is well drained. Tree peonies have sensitive roots, so be sure to amend the soil in and around the planting hole

To keep peonies blooming in the garden for an extended period, we planted early, mid-, and late-season bloomers, so throughout the season, some are in bud and about to bloom, while others are already in full blossom. Here, the herbaceous peony garden in Katonah is shown just a few weeks before bloom (top), buds straining at their seams. The 'Martha' variety (the name is a happy coincidence) is beautiful in bloom (bottom left) and in bud (bottom right).

with compost and, if the soil is acidic (pH scale between zero and 5.5), with lime; tree peonies prefer their sites slightly alkaline. The soil at the farm in Katonah has a pH of 6.5 to 7.0, which is ideal for growing peonies. We amend the soil there with superphosphate and Azomite, a natural product mined from ancient mineral deposits. These additives improve root systems and overall vigor, resulting in fantastic blooms.

LIGHT Full sunlight will yield the heftiest herbaceous peony blooms, so choose a location with direct sun—or dappled sun and shade all day. Sun-loving peonies will still flower when exposed to a little afternoon shade, and the blooms can last even longer. A place with protection from drying winds is also helpful; make sure there will be a lot of sun during the blooming season, mid-May to mid-June. Tree peonies can flourish in full sun or partial shade. They grow better and bloom more profusely in full sun, but the blossoms don't blow open as quickly when the plant is situated in some shade. Gardeners in warmer, southern zones (8 to 10) should choose sites in partial shade.

CHOOSING Herbaceous peony roots consist of the eyes (pink growth buds), crown or brain tissue, and root system full of stored energy. When choosing peonies, look for fleshy, firm roots (like firm carrots) and abundant eyes, as roots with at least three to five eyes (not too many sprouted) will acclimate best to new planting conditions. Unpack and examine the roots: look for a mass of thick roots that are not brittle; if dry, soak them in water for a few hours.

When we designed the peony garden, we concentrated on pink cultivars in masses; to date, we have more than twenty-two varieties in eleven double beds. Comprised of dozens of single, semidouble, double, and anemone-type blossoms, the peonies are from Klehm's Song Sparrow in Avalon, Wisconsin. To support the plants, a web of natural jute twine is woven crosswise and diagonally and threaded through the eyelet tops of aluminum stakes. The vast beds of the peony garden are surrounded by a double row of round and oval boxwoods.

PLANTING Always plant herbaceous peonies in the fall—as early as late August until November, about six weeks before the first frost is expected. Fall is also the best season to plant tree peonies, in order to encourage them to develop new roots and acclimate in time for normal growth the following spring. Spring-planted peonies may suffer for two to three years with lackluster blooms.

To plant, start by digging a hole 2 feet wide and deep. Turn the soil, and replace half of it with compost. Firm the soil at the bottom so the peony will not sink after planting, and then create a small mound of dirt and compost. Make sure the eyes are pointing upward and position the topmost eye just 2 inches below ground level. Spread the roots out over the mound you've created, and be sure to space plantings 3 to 4 feet apart for good air circulation. It's important to water thoroughly; you want to saturate the soil (pay attention to your soil type; clay or sandy soil may not drain efficiently)

and let the thirsty plant take a long drink.

When planting tree peonies, make sure the graft union (the point where the root meets the trunk) is about 1 inch below the soil. To support their boisterous growth, insert metal hoop guards into the soil, steering clear of roots. Cover soil with 2 inches of shredded-leaf or fine hardwood-bark mulch.

WATERING Water all types of peonies well during the first spring and summer (about an inch of water twice a week, depending on your climate and soil). In subsequent years, keep soil moist but not soggy during the growing season. Use your hands to test the soil below the surface; excess water will suffocate the roots, so do not water until the soil is dry underneath. Once established, tree peonies are very drought-tolerant plants.

FERTILIZING In early spring, when herbaceous peony plants are a foot tall, apply a fertilizer formulated for roses; feed again

From bud to full bloom, peonies are garden showstoppers. 'Rumpled Rose Ruffles' (above) is a showy tree peony that comes in various shades of pink. As the name implies, it has highly ruffled petals on a strong stem. For the longest life in an arrangement, cut stems of the herbaceous peony when the bud is still fairly tight. Day by day, the arrangement will change as petals unfurl and the inner carpel and stamens are exposed, as in these tree and hybrid peony blooms (opposite), including 'Anna Marie' and 'Leda' varieties.

after snipping off dead blooms. These formulations work just as well for peony plants, and can be used for tree peonies, as well—apply generously in the early autumn. In most regions, excepting truly arid climates, tucking in tree peonies with an additional blanket of organic mulch will ensure sufficient soil moisture through the winter. In the spring, add a light sprinkling of general fertilizer or compost; or, for young trees, drench them with fish emulsion.

PRUNING Don't leave faded flowers on your herbaceous peony plants, as they will sap the plant's energy and compromise the livelier blooms. Deadhead any spent flowers, along with a couple of inches of stem. As the plants die back to ground level, the leaves will slowly turn with the season; when they have completely browned, cut the stems to the ground, leaving only an inch or so (to help you remember where the plants are located).

It is important not to cut back tree peonies as you would herbaceous ones. Many years ago, there was a mix-up in my garden in Westport, and all the tree peonies were pruned to the ground. If this happens to you, know that while they'll never be trees again, they can grow back as bushy plants. In the meantime, make sure everyone who works in the garden knows the difference, and simply remove any fallen leaves from your tree peonies. Keep in mind that the trees set their buds in the late summer (into fall), so any cutting should be done right after they flower in order to prevent the loss of next season's blossoms. At Katonah, we prune the tree peonies to a height of 4 to 5 feet tall, only cutting dead wood and spent flowers, to let the blooms live at a comfortable eye level.

TROUBLESHOOTING If your peonies won't bloom, it's most likely due to improper planting depth, spring planting, or disease. When planting, make sure there's plenty of air circulation around the plant to help prevent fungal diseases like peony wilt, which can cause the foliage of both types of peonies to collapse and the flowers to die before opening. Watch your plants for spotted leaves, mushy stems, or blackened buds, which may indicate other fungal problems like botrytis blight. If you see symptoms, such as buds covered in a

fuzzy gray mold that spreads down the stem, remove infected portions, discard them, and clean your shears with alcohol. Thrips are another problem; these tiny pests damage buds and flowers by sucking their juices. To check for them, shake the buds over white paper—any small gray, brown, or yellow cigar-shaped insects are thrips. Remove and discard any affected buds.

Peonies are often associated with another insect: ants. The flower buds produce large quantities of nectar, and the attracted ants in turn provide protection against harmful insects. The ants won't harm the flowers (we have a small population that like the herbaceous peonies in Katonah). Simply use a gentle spray of water or shake off the insects before bringing any cut flowers inside.

HOW TO ARRANGE

CUTTING Herbaceous peonies make excellent cut flowers, and are best cut in bud form so they can open in the vase. Always cut flowers early in the morning or very late in the afternoon, when it's cool. Harvest buds when they are still fairly tight: you may see some cracks of color beginning to peek through, and the bud should feel like a firm marshmallow to the touch. "But, of course, when they're full blown," Kevin says, "they are at their most luscious; I try to pick them when they're budded but just about ready to pop." He recommends cutting the stems of herbaceous peonies as long as possible, and at an angle. These stems are sturdy, making them ideal for long, tall vessels and grand arrangements.

Handle tree peonies in an opposite manner: They have woody stems that must be cut very short. Cut the branch at a point between where the flower attaches and the leaves begin. You can sometimes include a leaf, but never cut a stem more than 2 to 4 inches long. This way, you'll avoid jeopardizing next year's crop of blossoms, and ensure that the cut flower will be able to draw up enough water. Tree peonies are excellent floated in bowls of water or placed in low arrangements.

MAINTAINING Peony arrangements can last up to a week or more if kept in a cool place and replenished with fresh water, so it's important to change the water daily. Be

Just-picked bicolor 'Dream Catcher' peonies in glorious full bloom are placed in tall collecting containers of water to keep them fresh. Yet the peonies look as lush and gorgeous as they would in any decorative vase, their sunny centers mirroring the pale yellow of the farm's signature Cantitoe Corners buckets. Casual yet elegant, they're a perfect addition to an outdoor table.

PEONY FORMS

Both tree and herbaceous peonies come in eight forms, or blossom shapes:

ANEMONE FORMS, with their many small petals, are low-growing (around 2 inches tall) and lightweight, so they don't require staking.

SINGLE-SHAPED PEONIES look like big daisies and are known for blooming prolifically. They have lots of stamens and a guard petal, and do well in afternoon shade.

LOTUS BLOSSOMS feature two or three layers of guard petals; they are sturdy flowers that don't need staking.

CHRYSANTHEMUM FORM blooms are many-petaled, with five to ten layers of guard petals that decrease in size as they approach the center. They prefer full sun and make great cut flowers.

ROSE PEONIES have hardly any stamens, many rows of petals, and even feature a rose-like scent.

GOLDEN CIRCLE FORMS have big, full flowers and are excellent in the vase.

CROWN BLOOMS feature large outer guard petals and tight, curly center petals; they're shaped like scoops of ice cream. When fully open, the guard petals fold all the way back to the stem.

HUNDRED PROLIFERATE PEONIES have the most petals—at least one hundred each, as the name indicates. They are so full that it is difficult to distinguish between guard and center petals.

---

aware that when petals start to drop, they tend to come off in clumps. Herbaceous peonies can also be stored when cut in bud form. Wrap them, dry, in newspaper—stems, buds, and all—and place them on their sides in the refrigerator for a month or longer. Keep them as dry as possible in storage, as any dampness can encourage fungus. For shorter-term storage, put the stems in water and wrap the rest in a plastic sleeve, then place in the fridge for up to a week. The buds will bloom when returned to room temperature.

ARRANGING Peony blossoms look equally lovely in bud form, half furled, or in full bloom, and you can include flowers in all of these various stages in your arrangement. Tight peony buds can lend a painterly accent to an arrangement, while full-blown peonies offer a sense of mass that can serve as a canvas for showing off other elements, such as the silhouette of a hosta leaf against a background of fluffy white blooms.

In springtime, the colorful buds of emerging peonies look especially beautiful with pale-pink tulips. Peonies can also pair well in arrangements with Siberian and bearded irises. In autumn, when the blooms are gone, mix the bronzed leaves with dark-colored

asters or dahlias. "I like to pair peonies with something that's smaller and more delicate, like fuchsia blossoms, or something airy, like smoke bush," Kevin notes, "because the smaller, daintier flowers allow you to appreciate how robust and gorgeous the peony blooms are. And peonies take up a lot of space in an arrangement, which not all flowers do, so they're useful on a large scale."

A mix of different varieties and shapes of peonies within an arrangement is especially nice, as they complement one another while providing a visual glossary of all their different forms. Peonies don't always need to be arranged en masse in order to make a statement; a giant tree peony blossom can make a visual impact all its own. Kevin's number one tip is not to forget about a flower's profile, especially when it comes to peonies. Most people think of a peony bloom only from directly above, but it can be just as beautiful in silhouette. "The crown-form 'Brother Chuck' white peony has always been one of my favorites; it has a cuff of outer petals that makes it look like a coconut macaroon, especially in profile."

These peonies' bright green stems play an architectural role in an arrangement that breaks convention, defying the common rule that the height of the arrangement must be equal to or taller than the vase. I bound the stems in a tight column with clear rubber bands, balancing the flowers' brilliant color against the delicate lines of a ginger-jar-shaped, silvered-glass vase. "Not all flowers have good-looking stems," Kevin says, "but peonies do." Just-unfurling buds add a nice roundness to the bouquet of 'Emma Klehm' variety blooms.

'Ivory Atlas' peonies, early bloomers with a double row of large, rounded petals, are set off with the tiny bell-like flowers of *Hyacinthoides hispanica* 'White City'. The delicate smaller flowers accentuate the robustness of the peonies and provide visual relief from the larger blooms. Feathery ferns and the strong greens of variegated hosta leaves lend this arrangement a woodland touch. To build, Kevin used a tape grid across the mouth of the vessel (see page 262), which gives the handful of peonies a boost, making them appear more numerous. He started by placing a cuff of hosta leaves around the outside of the vessel, then added the peonies, and finally the wood hyacinth.

OPPOSITE: A vintage black Chinese teapot with flower and dragon relief holds an arrangement of intensely saturated tree peonies with bright yellow centers. Kevin considers this arrangement a "step up" from floating a single blossom in a bowl, when you want to try something similar (short stems in a low, shallow vessel with a wide opening) but with a few extra layers. The lighter notes of *Dianthus*, placed at different heights for more variety, immediately draw the eye, the petal structure mimicking the appearance of moth wings. Kevin allowed the stems to remain long, which he says is a good way to make sure the little flowers don't get left behind.

The double-form 'Dayton' peony, with its cottage-garden friendly good looks, along with foamy sprays of smoke bush and sleek waves of dark *Heuchera* leaves, is right at home in a wicker basket. The texture of the willow-gathering container provides greater depth and tactility to the overall combination. Here, Kevin used a plastic liner and a brick of environmentally friendly floral foam, soaked for at least two hours until completely saturated. Once the floral foam was placed inside the vessel, he inserted the peonies and foliage interchangeably, to form undulating masses of flowers. "It's a toss-up as to who is the star of the show," he says. "Is it the peonies or the foliage?"

An exuberant gathering of mixed blush-colored peonies takes a tall midcentury Italian hand-painted pitcher to even greater heights. To offset the pastel ruffles of the 'Angel Cheeks' variety, sweeping amaranth is added, which provides movement and dimension to this bouquet. "You don't need to be an expert for this kind of arrangement," Kevin advises. "I just wanted this to be a pitcher filled with beautiful peonies." To help each blossom retain its shape and character, he chose peonies at different stages of bloom and cut their stems at varied lengths, then staggered them to best display the cuff of outer petals.

Inspired by an Old Master painting, Kevin arranged seasonal flowers in this French tureen. It is a true snapshot of the garden, containing all the flowers available at that very moment. The herbaceous peonies 'Brother Chuck', 'Elsa Sass', 'Prairie Moon', and 'Top Brass' mix well with 'Prize Gift' yellow tree peonies, columbine, wood hyacinth, trillium, and fuchsia. Green notes come from *Heuchera* and strawberry leaves. He started with a foundation of fluffy peonies, some of which become a little obscured in the final arrangement. "Flowers don't necessarily have to be seen in their complete, most beautiful condition to be successful in an arrangement."

If peonies symbolize good fortune, these 'Yellow Emperor' Itoh hybrid peonies seem destined to bring luck. Here, Kevin added very dark green and chartreuse hosta leaves and *Alchemilla* (lady's mantle) for shape and texture. "The leaves complemented the peonies' gorgeous, hot imperial yellow. Hostas are invaluable when it comes to flower arranging. They can add a splash of great color—variegated or solid—without stealing focus." He placed the hosta leaves first, then added the peonies one at a time. The *Alchemilla* came last, after analyzing the existing arrangement from multiple angles to discover where a little "noise" was needed.

The best companion plants play off the peonies' fragile, round prettiness: dark leaves and contrasting shapes. Here, a riotous mix of blood-red 'Cherry Charm' and 'Buckeye Belle' peonies, tropical bat-wing philodendron leaves, and foamy smoke bush sprigs contrasts with the refined tracery on a Wedgwood jasperware urn. A grid of clear plastic tape across the vase top supports the stems; Kevin built a foundation with the peonies, then added the leaves, and finished with smoke bush. *OPPOSITE*: To offset the 'Lafayette Escadrille' peonies in the deepest, most dramatic shades of red, frothy lady's mantle lightens up things and reflects the blossoms' sunny yellow centers. Spiky blades of *Carex* grass and chartreuse hosta provide contrasting texture and shape. "Chartreuse can be gorgeous in arrangements; it's a color I've really grown to appreciate since working with Martha," Kevin says. An antique salt-glazed stoneware storage jar gives the heady arrangement a simple, earthy base. "The lady's mantle adds that element of smoky fizz, and the *Carex* lends the sharpness that you need when arranging with big, fluffy peonies."

Marco Polo once likened peonies to "roses as big as cabbages." With their big blossoms, it doesn't take many peonies to form a perfect dome— and to make a lasting impression. Here, Kevin cut the stems of 'Miss Congeniality' anemone- form peonies short and massed them in a small but vibrant cloisonné bowl that plays on the flowers' off-the-charts color. "I took my cues from the container," he says. To construct the dome, he used a flower frog and started with the longest stem in the center. "I knew it would flop around a bit at the start," he explains, "but when you add the rest of the flowers in rings around the bowl, everything winds up where it needs to be."

The peony is such a strong foundation flower that it can be the base for an arrangement that builds up around it—or it can hold its own without too many supporting players. Here, Kevin matched white bomb-form peonies with ferns, catalpa blooms, and the arching stems of Solomon's seal in a hand-painted, bottle-shaped porcelain vase by Ruth Gurvich, a Paris-based Argentinean artist. "The arrangement is a nice sort of conversation among blooms on different scales," Kevin says.

Summer's Bounty

In each of my gardens, lots of things happen in summertime. In Katonah, the farm heats up quickly and everything just dries up. It took only two years until I understood why so many of my neighbors left town and summered elsewhere. It can become very stifling in the area, as it is landlocked and the elevation is not very high. Watering the gardens is essential; constant deadheading is also very important. Vegetables grow extremely well, but flowers can become leggy and lank in these less-than-optimal conditions. Still, I can grow fine annuals, and the later-blooming perennials, such as lilies, can bloom profusely if watered at ground level.

Maine is another story altogether. Many people from the New York area, Boston, and Philadelphia go to Maine to find cool nights, warm days, ocean breezes, and other such comforts. My plants there perform extremely well all summer, but August is the month for gardens to show off. Everything in Maine, all flowers and vines, are for August show. My birthday is on August 3, and I can be sure that my terrace beds and cutting gardens are full of colorful and extraordinary flowers from the last week in July through the third week in August.

Warm dry days, cool short nights, and sufficient

SEASONAL
ALL-STARS

ROSE
POPPY
CLEMATIS
DELPHINIUM
HYDRANGEA
LILY

Summer is the season of constant bloom and rich color in the cutting garden. When one variety ends its blooming period, another takes its place. Poppies are followed by many varieties of lilies and Siberian iris, which lead to hollyhocks and gladioli.

rainfall make gardening there a real joy. And almost everyone partakes in the homekeeping pleasure of gardening. Pots are filled with showy, tuberous begonias; cacti, aloes, agaves, and cycads, also in pots, thrive during the long, hot days; and lilies and delphiniums grow to amazing heights. One lily a few years ago grew to 8 feet tall and displayed no fewer than forty-five flowers on its stem. I cut it and gave it to my dear friend David Rockefeller, then ninety-nine years old, knowing that he would appreciate such a rare and beautiful specimen.

Another attractive feature of the summer gardens at Skylands in Maine is that they are celebrated with garden tours and lectures, which are all very well attended by garden enthusiasts.

In East Hampton, the summer gardens are also moderated well by the ocean's proximity and the cooler coastal climate. There are great blooms in the flowerbeds but also in the borders, where the colorful hydrangeas start to bloom in August and continue well into fall. Lilies, clematis, zinnias, gladioli, asters, and sweet William abound. Farm stands are bright and colorful with hundreds of flower bouquets cut daily from the productive fields nearby. No one can resist buying flowers by the armload, as they are so plentiful and fine.

OTHER SEASONAL
HIGHLIGHTS

FOXGLOVE
SWEET WILLIAM
HOLLYHOCK
SWEET PEA
SNAPDRAGON
GLADIOLA
ZINNIA
AMARANTHUS
ASTER

LEFT: Zinnias are such easy-care annuals that they're great for beginning gardeners. Just give them plenty of sun and well-drained soil. Kevin made a chromatic all-zinnia arrangement in a huge bowl, grouping the various reds, such as 'State Fair', 'Queen Red Lime', and 'Benary's Giant Wine', in a dome (see page 274 for more on domes). *RIGHT:* A narrow vase of foxgloves (*Digitalis*) allows an appreciation of each individual flower, the speckled throats of their petals on full display. Dramatic and richly colored, foxgloves grow straight and tall in the garden, and will continue to stand at attention in a vibrant arrangement.

Lupine is another beautifully textured spiky flower that comes in saturated shades beyond the familiar purple. They can bloom from May through July; in mid-June, I love seeing vast fields of lupines in Maine. Here, their pea-shaped florets are mirrored in the hobnail glass pitcher, along with hellebores and variegated hosta leaves.
OPPOSITE: It's simple to make easygoing zinnias look elegant: Use a sophisticated vase. Kevin assembled a large collection of flowers in many colors in this Chinese porcelain urn, holding them in place with a tape grid (see page 262).

The wavy form of snapdragons is part of their allure. When they are immersed at an angle in water, an even greater curve develops in their stem, which can add interesting lines to an arrangement. To do this, Kevin positions the flowers diagonally (so they're almost horizontal) in a wide bucket of water overnight. In this arrangement of pale flowers, he let some snapdragons drape over the edge and others stand upright, and punctuated the look with dark sunflowers to add the illusion of deep spaces within. *OPPOSITE*: Gladioli in several shades have a sharper profile when some of the stems are in bloom and others still in bud. Their impressive size is played up in this large glazed ginger jar.

Everyday flowers are elevated once placed in a silver vessel. Petite, bicolored sweet William and bright carnations form a base for (and peek through the layers of) soaring lupine and foxglove. Kevin used a cage frog in the vase, working his way from the smaller flowers to the largest blooms. *OPPOSITE:* Delicate sweet peas grow in clusters, so they look best arranged in a natural fashion, here bunched together in a clear-glass footed compote.

This abundant arrange-
ment lets it all hang
out: single, double,
fully-double, and
clustered form roses
mix with 'Ballerina',
spilling over the edges
of a nineteenth-century
American pressed-glass
footed bowl. (A com-
pote, sugar bowl, and
pair of eggcups placed
alongside complete
the display.) In a wide-
mouthed vessel like
this one, use a floral
frog secured in place
with floral gum. A tape
grid (see page 262) is
also effective for making
fewer flowers look abun-
dant. Here, the many
shades of pink and the
myriad textures create
a sense of movement.
Kevin positioned the
larger roses first, then
worked his way down
in size to the smallest.

Rose

ROSA

MY INTEREST IN ROSES BEGAN MANY YEARS AGO IN MY PATERNAL GRANDMOTHER'S ROSE GARDEN IN NUTLEY, NEW JERSEY. BABCIA HELEN GREW HYBRID TEA ROSES IN A RICH BED THAT MEASURED ABOUT 10 FEET BY 40 FEET. SHE WAS VERY FRUGAL, AND RATHER THAN PURCHASE A ROSEBUSH OF A TYPE SHE ADMIRED, SHE LEARNED TO PROPAGATE ROSES FROM CUTTINGS.

Her method was simple—take cuttings, remove most of their leaves, and insert them, four or five in a circle, in her garden soil, under a large glass mayonnaise or pickle jar. Grandma's roses were quite famous. For presents, she would give rooted plants to her three children, and we grandchildren coveted blooms to take to our teachers because we knew that her tea roses, especially those of the 'Peace' variety, were the largest and best in the neighborhood.

Grandma did not have rooting hormone to help her propagation process, but she certainly knew how to feed, water, and prune rosebushes. A barrel of manure "tea" stood right by the garden, and she never let the bushes get thirsty. The leaves were surprisingly disease-free; I don't recall any signs of black spot or yellowing, but I do remember that soapy water, tobacco water, and coppery-green solutions were applied

> "ROSES ARE ATTRACTIVE FOR THEIR
> FREE-GROWING HABITS, THEIR ENDLESS
> VARIETY, THEIR DELECTABLE
> PERFUME, AND THE EASE WITH WHICH
> THEY SEEM TO THRIVE."

regularly. Japanese beetles didn't stand a chance, with her nimble fingers plucking off offenders and dropping them into a jar of kerosene.

My father, too, grew almost everything from seeds or cuttings, and his vision was more expansive than Grandma's. Dad dreamed and he studied, and he started me on my quest for different kinds of roses. He planted our front walk in Nutley with a border of 'Tropicana' roses. I always complained that I didn't like their colors— oranges, yellows, and corals—but Dad thought that they, of all roses, would do the best there. He encouraged me to enter "our" roses in local flower shows, and, after several blue ribbons from the Nutley Women's Club, I became a rose addict. When I moved to Westport, Connecticut, my husband and daughter gave me twelve wonderful tea rosebushes one Mother's Day, and I was on my way to serious collecting. After the teas, I started to accumulate scores of old roses. I was attracted by their free-growing habits, their endless variety, their delectable perfume, and the ease with which they seemed to thrive. I visited Sissinghurst and Mottisfont Abbey in England, and Giverny in France, and I craved knowledge about the kinds of roses I saw there—shrub roses, *centifolias*, Bourbons, and hybrid perpetuals.

When I began my East Hampton garden, I knew much more about which roses I loved and those I could live without. I knew which roses bloomed only once and then turned into a huge green shrub, never to bloom again that year. Still, I couldn't resist planting the apricot 'Alchymist' and the pink 'Raubritter', despite their ill-mannered once-flowering nature. In 2013, I transplanted the roses from East Hampton (more than 350 bushes!) to Katonah, and I am delighted by how well they survived the trip. Every single bush is thriving, and I look forward to another prodigious show this summer, and for many years to come. I do wish my father could see the progress I've made as a gardener. And I would be so happy if he could smell the wonderful profusion of roses on the farm. He would certainly be gratified that his early encouragement and teaching made me so willing—and successful—a student.

Morning dew collects on the blossoms of 'Excellenz von Shubert', a double-flowered rose. The double varieties often display various shades of color as they open from tight bulbs to full-blown flowers. In general, the more petals a rose has, the more perfumed it is.

GROWING
& ARRANGING

A ROSE IS A ROSE, OF COURSE, BUT THE FLOWERS COME IN SO MANY COLORS, TYPES, SHAPES, SCENTS, AND FORMS THAT EVERY GARDENER IS BOUND TO FIND A VARIETY WELL SUITED TO HIS OR HER PARTICULAR SITE, CLIMATE, AND GARDEN. AND THE POSSIBILITIES FOR ARRANGING ARE NEARLY AS LIMITLESS.

HOW TO GROW

Roses can be single- or double-flowered, pale or dark, and grown on dense bushes or airy vines. The roses at Skylands begin their season in early spring, when the gardeners and I remove the burlap enclosures they had placed around each bed at the start of winter (see Overwintering, page 143; it's milder in Katonah, so the roses there don't require the burlap). The profusion of blooms each summer is well worth that extra step.

ZONE Roses are best grown in Zones 4 to 10, depending on the variety. They are regional plants, and each class or species prefers a certain climate. For example, *Gallica* roses, part of a class perfected in nineteenth-century France, have proven both winter hardy and disease-resistant in my New York gardens (and in my Connecticut garden years ago). In the Southeast, however, *Gallica* is a poor choice; you'll find better results with tea, China, or hybrid musk roses. Along the Pacific coast, hybrid tea and *Floribunda* roses thrive— and still others, such as *Alba* roses, can perform as well in the cold Maine air as in the heat of Los Angeles.

SOIL Roses flourish in sites with well-drained soil that is loaded with organic material. If your soil is sandy or full of clay, add compost and manure and mix well. This produces a medium that drains efficiently but also holds enough moisture for the plants to drink. Mulch also makes growing roses easier, as it helps the soil stay cool and moist during hot weather, cutting down on the need to water. It also inhibits many common weeds, and, when made from organic matter such as bark, grass clippings, manure, straw, or leaves, should break down over time and improve the quality of your soil.

LIGHT Plant roses where they can get at least six hours of direct sun every day. If they can get eight to ten hours, that's ideal, as it will promote better blooming. Dark-red and black roses, though, can stand a bit of afternoon shade so they don't burn. Climbing roses will do some of the work on their own; to clamber upward and reach sunlight, they take advantage of their thorns' natural propensity to hook onto anything nearby. Lend your climbers a hand by adding a trellis or other structure that they can grab on to.

CHOOSING Rose plants can be purchased either in pots or in bare-root, dormant form. Both are good as long as they're from reputable growers; if you're new to roses, try both and see which you prefer. Mail-order plants are almost always sold bare-root, which offers a wider variety, especially many older rose varieties that are only available through specialty nurseries. Look for bare-root plants that feel heavy (a lightweight

I have a large variety of roses growing in Katonah, including vigorous climbing roses, which are exceptionally versatile. The extra length and pliability of their canes make them a dramatic covering for rock walls and fences, and they furnish living architecture when trained on trellises and arbors. Here, a massive bank of rambling roses has taken over the back fence between the chicken coop and the pumpkin patch.

root means it is dried out) and that have thicker, smooth canes (stems). They should be brownish-green, not tan-colored; avoid those coated in wax.

PLANTING To plant a bare-root rose, dig a hole approximately 18 inches wide and 18 inches deep and form a conical mound at the bottom of the hole. Ensure the mound is the right height by positioning the root on the soil so the bud union sits on top and the roots extend down over the mound. In warmer climates, the bud union should be at or just above ground level. In colder places, it should be 1 inch to 2 inches below ground level. Once you've determined the correct height of the mound, remove the root, add some rose food (follow package instructions), and replace. Fill the hole with soil, making sure there are no air spaces among the roots, and water thoroughly. For a first planting, mound soil around the planting and create a moat around the bush. Water again, thoroughly. The moat will help prevent water from running off and ensure it reaches the roots.

WATERING Most roses grow best if they get about an inch of water each week during the growing season, depending on soil type. Gardeners with sandy soil often find their roses need a little more water than those with soil high in clay. To gauge your sprinkler's effectiveness, set out empty cans to time how long it takes an inch of water to collect.

Always water in the morning so that the plants can dry before nightfall, which will help ward off fungal diseases that can result from damp foliage. With that in mind, never water plants from above. For a large rose garden or in places where water is scarce, soaker hoses, which slowly seep water directly at ground level, or drip irrigation systems are the best watering tools. Because they release water a drop at a time, they're less likely to create runoff, and they apply water directly to the soil, which makes them better for irrigating plants that are prone to foliar diseases (those affecting the leaves).

FERTILIZING After the burlap is removed from my Skylands rosebushes and the crowns are uncovered each spring, I form a saucer, or well, of the compost around each bush to facilitate watering. Depending on its size and age, we give each plant a half to one cup of Epsom salts and one cup of Rose-tone, a packaged fertilizer high in organic ingredients. Every two weeks during the bud and blooming stages, they are fed with liquid seaweed and fish emulsion (available at garden supply stores). The soil is rejuvenated with a couple of inches of compost in spring and fall. In the fall in Katonah, and again each March, I sprinkle a half to one cup of Epsom salts around each plant, and allow the rain (or snow!) to melt it into the soil. I also like to spread coffee grounds around the base of the rosebushes throughout the year, especially in the spring to promote abundant growth. (I collect them from the Martha Stewart Café in the lobby of my office building.) As a general rule, I don't use fungicide or pesticide sprays preventively—only if problems occur.

PRUNING In springtime, remove the three Ds (anything dead, damaged, or diseased), and remember that pruning isn't just for "pruning season." Feel free to shape your roses all season long, as you would any other plant in your garden—while you are deadheading is a great time (see below). To protect your hands and arms from thorns, wear leather gloves and a heavy, long-sleeved shirt. Disinfect pruners between cuts (on different plants) by dipping the blades in a mixture of one part household bleach to ten parts water. This prevents disease from spreading from plant to plant. As a rule of thumb, don't reduce the height of most garden roses by more than a third. For spring- and summer-flowering varieties, do not prune again until after they have bloomed. Leave at least three or four strong, outward-growing canes (stems) on each plant. For climbing roses, cut back their horizontal side branches by half after flowering.

Deadheading is the process by which spent or fading flowers are cut from their stems. It is done for aesthetic purposes— to eliminate unsightly dead blooms from the garden—as well as for practical ones. By removing a spent flower, you are also removing the plant's immature seeds, thereby saving the plant from focusing its energy on seed production. A deadheaded rosebush will concentrate its energies on food production and storage, and, in some cases, on the

This view of the porch at my home on Lily Pond Lane, in East Hampton, shows some of the many antique roses I planted there. Of the several hundred varieties I chose, most were Old Garden roses, and the rest had the look, if not the pedigree. They bloomed in waves from May to late October, many climbing over trellises and porches, as in an English country garden. In 2013, I transplanted the shrub roses (many of them more than two decades old and weakened) to Katonah, where they were brought back to vigor and beauty.

production of another round of blooms. If your roses are the type that bloom only once in a season, such as Damasks, deadheading cleans up the look of the bush; if you have repeat-bloomers such as *rugosas* or hybrid teas, deadheading will help the plants to continue producing abundant flowers. When you're ready to remove a flower, make your cut just above the first cluster of five leaflets on the stem below the bloom—any higher and you run the risk of hurting the next round of blooms. Use only sharp, clean bypass pruners, which make precise cuts and allow the stem to heal properly, thereby reducing the risk of infection by bacteria and other plant pathogens.

As beneficial as deadheading can be, it is important to know when to stop. It is only by allowing flowers to remain on their stems at the end of the season that rose hips—the fruits of the rosebush that provide attractive winter color in the garden—have a chance to appear. If you live in a cool climate, it's also a good idea to stop deadheading in the late summer and let the plant go dormant naturally. Pushing roses to continue blooming when the weather turns cool can be stressful for the plants, leaving them ill-equipped to withstand the winter's chillier temperatures.

OVERWINTERING If you live in a northern region, you will probably need to protect your roses during the winter, which is essentially the process of making sure they stay frozen until spring. Rosebushes are frequently damaged by changes in temperature—one day the soil freezes, the next it thaws—which causes "heaving" of the soil. This pushes the plant's roots to the surface, leaving them vulnerable to the cold and causing them to dry out. There are a few common methods to overwinter your roses; whichever one you choose, wait until the soil has frozen before beginning the process. The first is using mulch: Cover rose canes with 4 to 5 inches of loose mulch, such as weed-free straw, leaf mulch, pine needles, or wood chips.

Protect roses in extremely cold areas with rose cones, foam devices that resemble white traffic cones. Mound soil over the crown, and then cover the entire plant with the cone. Cut a few ventilation holes, and anchor it so it won't blow away during winter storms.

Another method is growing roses in large containers and moving them to a sheltered spot for the winter—such as an unheated garage, storage shed, or cool basement.

At Skylands, which has rough Maine winters, we wrap burlap around the entire rose garden to protect the plants from the elements. After the plants are top-dressed in late autumn, wooden stakes are pounded into the soil about 5 feet apart, and lengths of 36-inch-wide burlap are stapled to the stakes. When the ground freezes, we spread salt hay in fluffy mounds atop the soil to prevent heaving and to provide extra insulation. The hay is secured with baling twine criss-crossed between bamboo stakes to keep it from blowing away. Come spring, the hay is removed and saved for next year's service. Winters are milder in Katonah (Zone 5 to 6, depending on the year), so we don't wrap the roses but simply add a few inches of compost to each plant to protect the crown.

Remember that the best defense against winter damage to your roses is a good offense. Make sure that your rosebushes are properly nourished throughout the growing season and that any parasites and diseases are controlled. This will help your plants keep their leaves, which will improve their chances of winter survival.

TROUBLESHOOTING Roses are commonly attacked by a number of fungal diseases, including black spot, powdery mildew, and rust. Black spot is caused by the fungus *Diplocarpon rosae*, which invades the vascular tissue of leaves, resulting in unsightly black areas. The leaves yellow and eventually drop; in time, the plants can become virtually defoliated. Light black spot at season's end is almost inevitable, but not harmful—it is the extreme and untreated cases that can mortally weaken plants.

Affected roses can often be coaxed into recovery with nonchemical treatments. One do-it-yourself option is to spray every five to ten days with a mixture of four teaspoons baking soda and one tablespoon horticultural oil per gallon of water. Spray only in the early morning or after heavy rains, as the treatment has the potential to burn leaves if applied during the hottest part of the day. Another option is to treat with an antitranspirant, or antidesiccant—normally

It's best to cut roses first thing in the morning, when it's cool. I collect the flowers, such as this mix of varieties at Lily Pond, in a wicker gathering basket, then promptly put them in cold or lukewarm water to keep them from wilting. Before I begin arranging the roses, I use a sharp knife to clean the stems and strip them of their thorns. Kevin stresses the importance of choosing roses that also have healthy, beautiful foliage, which can serve as a buffer in an arrangement that combines several types.

used to prevent plants from experiencing excessive water loss, they can form a barrier between leaf pores and invading black-spot fungi. And whole neem oil, a substance derived from the seeds of the tropical neem tree and available at nurseries and garden supply stores, also helps prevent and control black spot. Use two tablespoons of 90 percent whole neem oil per gallon of warm water, spraying according to directions.

Ultimately, preemptive measures to ensure strong plants are the best way to keep roses healthy. Plant roses in open, sunny, and breezy locations, and practice good garden hygiene by keeping the plants well pruned and removing fallen leaves, diseased canes, and garden litter from beds. Thinning plants promotes good circulation and helps avoid the humid conditions that breed fungus spores. You can also choose cultivars that have natural defenses. Developed before the modern age of chemical sprays, Old Garden roses such as the *Gallica*, Damask, and *Alba* varieties (all of which I grow) tend to be more naturally resistant to disease and pests than some of the newer hybrids.

HOW TO ARRANGE

CUTTING Roses can be cut at all different stages of bloom, depending on what kind of arrangement you have in mind. Tightly budded roses are quietly appealing, partial blooms are likely to open slowly, and fully blown blossoms can make for real show-stopping arrangements.

Use sharp, clean cutters and trim the rose stems at an angle so that they do not sit flat on the bottom of the vase, which can impede water intake. For very woody-stemmed varieties, it can be beneficial to crosshatch (cut into the stem in an X pattern) the end of the branch so as to draw up more water. Promptly put the cut flowers in a bucket of lukewarm water (or cold water if you want them to remain at the bud stage longer). Kevin likes to give the flowers at least half an hour to soak; you can even let them soak overnight. It is worth the effort to remove the thorns. Use a stem stripper (see page 261) or a sharp knife, and be patient. Some varieties will be thornier than others. (Don't cut thorns from the actual plant, however; the wounds would allow insects and disease access.) On a

rosebush, you can have a veritable bounty of roses, and there's no reason not to cut a lot of them for display. When you snip existing blossoms, the plant diverts energy into the production of new flowers. So the more you cut, the more it will bloom.

MAINTAINING Roses are fairly hardy when treated well; they will last a long time as a cut flower, especially when cut in bud form. They benefit from regularly changing the water—even more so than other flowers—and they don't attract any particular kind of pests. If choosing roses from outside of your own garden, make sure that the buds are not extremely tight and smooth, like onions. This generally means that the guard petals have been pulled off and the rose is essentially denuded; it would be like buying a head of lettuce without any lettuce leaves.

ARRANGING Cage frogs work well when arranging roses, because the stems are rarely consistent or uniform. Pay close attention to the stem, as it will dictate how that bloom can be used in an arrangement. For example, a huge, beautiful rose might be growing on a very slight, weak stem. Don't try to fight it; instead, choose an arrangement and a vessel that can work with the stem you have.

Rose arrangements can be surprisingly versatile, as there are so many varieties of roses to choose from. And they can go in almost any container, depending on how many blooms you have and of which varieties. Some go-tos for Kevin and me are bubble bowls or trumpets. Kevin also loves a singular rose with a perfect leaf in a slim bud vase. An arrangement of many different types can look so diverse that you may not even recognize them all as roses. Even within a color family, there are so many hues of red or pink to highlight; mix different shades of crimson to accentuate the flower's many moods. Match pale colors with saturated hues to make the brights pop, or group pastels to show off the differences in petal variety. To add interest to a yellow bouquet, throw in a stem of orange or pink. Don't forget about the leaves; add a border of foliage to highlight the colors of the petals, and let the vessel's lip support the weight of slender leaf stems.

A palette of rosy hues brings roses and yarrow together and creates a spectrum of shapes, from tiniest floret to full-blown bloom. Using a classic garden ornament, like this cast-iron urn in East Hampton, reinforces the idea of bringing the outdoors in. Kevin placed a ball of chicken wire in the urn to hold the stems securely, allowing him to create an extra-tall and -wide arrangement.

Blowsy roses are those big blooms that are just a touch past their peak. They're glorious in their fullness and fragrance. Here, Kevin used a tape grid over a sawtooth-pattern pressed-glass trumpet vase to bring together a group of pale-pink roses from the Skylands garden, along with lady's mantle, interspersed among the roses to give the arrangement variety and "fizz."

OPPOSITE: Fragrance and texture combine in this grouping of *Floribunda* roses, jasmine, hellebore, and geranium leaves at Skylands. To keep the scent of the bouquet from being overpowering, it contains fewer roses than an arrangement this size otherwise could. A stout vessel from my collection of faux bois—its handle mimics a branch wrapping around a tree trunk—provides earthy balance.

KEVIN SHARKEY

Everyone has some kind of relationship to roses—you've either given or received them, and you're bound to have a favorite.

Do you have a favorite rose?

I like tea roses, and Martha loves Old Garden roses. I've always loved red roses, especially with the green leaves attached—the colors complement each other so well. And then there are climbers: I remember the first time I went to Martha's house in East Hampton, where her primary rose garden was, and I was blown away by the fact that she had trained climbing roses to go up the pear trees on the property. They looked like rose trees, because blooming vines were growing out of every branch. I'd never seen anything like it; it was such an incredible idea.

What do you pair with roses?

I love looking at just one rose, or a lot of them. Roses sometimes seem to me as if they don't want to be with any other flowers: Just let the roses be with the roses. However, some varieties, especially spray roses, are beautiful when mixed in with other things. And I really appreciate the leaves on roses. They can help tie multicolor bouquets together and they're an excellent shade of green (see opposite). That's part of the reason why a single rose with its own leaf can be so perfectly

beautiful. I like roses paired with lots of greenery; when I don't use their own foliage, I also like geranium leaves or ferns. As an arranger, you should pay as much attention to the leaves as you do the flowers.

What are some rules on color?

I generally prefer to keep rose arrangements monochromatic (see page 135)—but that's not to say a multicolor bouquet can't be beautiful. The important thing is to keep the color temperature at the forefront of your mind. Two roses may not mesh, even if they're both red: A warm-hued red and a cool, blue-toned red won't sit well together. Keep mixed colors in the same temperature family, even when it comes to white roses. If you pay attention to whether it's a warm white or a cool white, it can really lift the color profile and provide some breathing room in a dense arrangement. But the wrong color white can throw everything off—think about how a colorful umbrella can cast a slightly "off" color onto the face of the person holding it. A white rose can sometimes cause odd color effects in the surrounding blooms, so when in doubt, skip the white roses in mixed-color arrangements.

Any common mistakes when arranging roses?

I do not endorse *Gypsophila*, commonly known as baby's breath. The easiest thing you can do to make a rose arrange-

ment 200 percent better is to take the baby's breath out of it. I love baby's breath, but it just doesn't flatter roses. It changes the scale. I think sometimes people underestimate the approachability of roses—they have a reputation for being formal. But they look just as nice in a galvanized bucket as they do in a cut-glass bowl.

Any tricks for arranging roses?

The great thing about roses is they are incredibly versatile. A rose can be the star of an arrangement or a bunch can be used as filler flowers. They're another flower I like to cut in all different stages—the tightly budded ones can be so pretty, and of course the full blooms are gorgeous. Some varieties have more thorns than others—you can use a stem stripper (see page 261), but most of the time, I just use a knife or my hands.

I find cage frogs to be the most helpful for arranging. The stems are not consistent from rose to rose, so a cage helps to corral many different shapes and sizes. It's always better to let the stem dictate what the flower can do—you might have the biggest, most beautiful flower head that you want to make the focus of your arrangement, but you may not be able to place it exactly how you envisioned. Don't try to fight it—just value-engineer your arrangement into what the stems are telling you.

For greater impact than a single arrangement can provide, pair up colors and leaves in identical vases. These *Gallica versicolors* are among my favorite varieties of roses, for their exuberant striped blooms and beautiful fragrance. In this instance, Kevin paired them with white 'Fair Bianca' and red 'Charles de Mille' roses, along with a few of their healthiest dark green leaves, in English free-blown flip glasses, giving the arrangement a feeling of greater abundance and contrast. "When some flowers drop their petals, you want to brush them away," Kevin says. "But rose petals can be left beneath the arrangement for a day."

Use your imagination when choosing a vessel for roses. Think about repurposing something unexpected. Here, Kevin filled a shiny copper pudding mold with 'Cardinal de Richelieu' roses and accented them with delicate Indian painted ferns. These roses grow with many blossoms on a single branch; their short stems allow for an opportunity to use a more petite container.

OPPOSITE: This rare pink mercury-glass rose bowl reflects the room and the light on the staircase at Lily Pond. A pedestal elevates the arrangement and suits the narrow stairway landing. Combining *Gallica versicolor* and solid-color roses adds dimension to the mix, and fine-leaved, wispy *Cotinus* (smoke bush) lightens the display.

An unadorned apothecary jar holds a pale cluster of single, double, and full-form white and blush-pink roses, punctuated with buds. Kevin created a tape grid over the mouth of the jar to more easily position the roses in concentrated areas and hold them in place.

OPPOSITE: A straightforward dome of pink roses can take an artful turn with the addition of a few unexpected elements. Dusty-yellow roses with smoky centers, the patterned petals of bell-shaped fritillaria, and the pink carnations and jasmine vine reach outward to extend the arrangement, held in place by the classic shape of the bubble bowl, with its narrow mouth. Choosing an opaque vessel eliminates the need to arrange the stems perfectly. The bowl's rose-gold color accentuates the scheme of the arrangement.

Poppy

PAPAVER

MY FATHER GREW POPPIES IN HIS GARDEN IN NUTLEY, NEW JERSEY. I LOVED THEM AND I WAITED WHILE THE OVOID FUZZY GREEN BUDS SEGMENTED IN PIECES AND UNFURLED INTO PAPERY, BRILLIANT ORANGE AND RED AND APRICOT FLOWERS EACH YEAR. I KNEW I WOULD ALWAYS HAVE POPPIES IN MY GARDEN, AND I PLANTED LOTS IN MY FIRST BIG GARDEN AT TURKEY HILL.

I was particularly fond of one type of unnamed poppy, a pale orange double poppy with petals thinner than the sturdy large Oriental poppies we all know and love, but graceful and nodding on wavy stems, self-sowing, and spreadable. My neighbor Fred Specht gave me a few plants, and I encouraged and nurtured them for years. When I left Westport, and that garden with all its treasure, I vowed to come back to get some of those poppies. Yet in fifteen years, I still have not yet managed to grow any of that type at the farm in Katonah, and I need them and want them desperately.

There are many kinds and colors of poppies, and somewhere between fifty and one hundred species, but only four of those species actually make it into most perennial gardens: *Papaver somniferum,* or opium poppy; *Papaver rhoeas* or Flanders, Shirley,

or corn poppy; *Papaver nudicaule,* or Icelandic poppy; and most important, *Papaver orientale* or Oriental poppy. True perennials, Oriental poppies are valued for color and shape in most home gardens, ranging from white to many shades of orange, to pink, rose, lavender, crimson, raspberry, and even dark red.

Annie's Annuals & Perennials catalog, from the company based in Richmond, California, offers some exotic poppies, including annuals such as *P. rhoeas* 'Falling in Love', hybrid poppy 'Orange Chiffon', and a perennial Moroccan poppy called 'Flore Pleno', an always blooming, hardy pale-orange flower. Many poppies have extraordinary embellishments, such as fringed petals, feathered petals, splotched petals, and shaded petals, and all have abundant, pollen-bearing anthers and somewhat bristly stems and leaves. The bread poppy, grown for its seeds used in baking, and the opium poppy have smoother, more succulent foliage.

Most poppies are not considered a fine or long-lasting cut flower, but I still incorporate them into arrangements because of their colors and gracefulness. To prolong their life once cut, it's essential to first sear the stem's end immediately in a hot flame to seal the latex sap that exudes from the wounded stem. Depending on where you garden, plant as many of these lovely flowers as possible. The annuals often seed themselves the following year, and the perennials, if well tended, can be expected to live a good long life.

In the Katonah garden in late June, sunshine highlights the veins in the whisper-thin ruffled petals of the opium or breadseed poppy (*P. somniferum*).

GROWING
& ARRANGING

*WITH THEIR DELICATE PETALS AND BOISTEROUS GOOD
LOOKS, YOU MIGHT EXPECT POPPIES TO BE DIFFICULT TO GROW.
YET ALMOST ANY BRIGHT, SUNNY BED OR OPEN FIELD
SHOULD ACCOMMODATE POPPIES, AND AN ARRANGEMENT OF
THESE FLOWERS ALWAYS DRAWS ATTENTION.*

HOW TO GROW

Poppies have wide single or double cups, with very thin petals that may be fringed, feathered, or splotched. The broad color palette includes all shades of white, purple, pink, and red, as well as glowing hues, like my favorite, a dark glowing orange Oriental poppy. (And for a true blue, there's another species entirely, *Meconopsis betonicifolia* [see page 181], which is extremely difficult to grow in most of North America.)

ZONE Different species of poppies can be grown in zones ranging from 2 to 9 (see page 160); be sure to choose the variety best suited to your climate.

SOIL Poppies like moist, well-drained, friable soil. "Friable"' means that when you squeeze it, the soil should hold together for a brief moment and then unclump on its own. To make your soil more friable, add plenty of organic matter (compost, raked leaves, grass clippings, coffee grounds) to amend the consistency, and work it in thoroughly with a spade or tiller.

LIGHT All species of poppies need plenty of sun, at least six to eight hours per day.

CHOOSING Poppies can be planted from seed or already-germinated seedlings, available at nurseries and garden centers. (If this

is your second season of poppies, however, the choice may not be up to you: the ripened seed heads will self-sow and take root just about anywhere, even on steep hillsides or in sparse soil between pathway stones.) If planting seedlings, make sure they are in biodegradable pots, as poppies are resistant to transplanting—Icelandic and some Oriental varieties are most adaptable. Look for young plants with a number of flower stems and unopened buds; skip any that have yellowed leaves, which can be an indication of root rot. Check the crown of the plant where the foliage meets the roots, and avoid any that appear soft or mushy.

PLANTING For successive blooms, sow the seeds repeatedly from early spring well into late summer. If the climate where you live is mild, sow poppies in the fall for early spring germination. To fill in foliage gaps left by summer-dormant species such as Oriental poppies, grow them among later-flowering perennials. At the farm in Katonah, I plant mine in mixed borders or scattered throughout the cutting garden.

Due to their tiny, specklike size, poppy seeds can be challenging to place exactly where you want them. The seeds can be black, white, brown, gray, or tan, and some gardeners mix them with light-colored sand in order to better see them. For a quick and easy

Poppies bloom for only about two weeks in early summer, and their brief season is something to celebrate at the Katonah farm. To get successive blooms, we sow seeds from early spring to late summer. In addition to (clockwise from top left) 'Lauren's Grape', Flanders poppy, and 'French Flounce' shown here, we grow many varieties of Icelandic, California, and breadseed poppies.

planting technique in a large area, pierce small holes in the lid of a jam jar, combine three parts sand with one part seeds in the jar, and use as a seed shaker, sprinkling at will. This will help keep the seeds separated and less likely to clump too close together, potentially saving some effort when thinning the plants later. Sow seeds roughly 1 inch apart, and do not cover—it is very important that they receive light in order to germinate. Simply scatter on the soil surface and lightly scratch into the dirt. Water carefully with a watering can or a hose with a misting nozzle. When the poppies have reached a height of 3 to 4 inches, you may need to thin them. The seeds and seedlings are so tiny and numerous that they will grow too thickly if left alone.

Pinch out clusters as the plants grow in order to prevent them from strangling one another. Continue pinching until you reach your desired number.

WATERING Although poppies are drought-resistant, deep watering promotes the development of a strong root system. Take care not to water too frequently, as the root crowns of poppies can rot easily, and blight or fungus can decimate the leaves. Poppies need good drainage; avoid waterlogged soil.

PRUNING With poppies other than Oriental types, cut down as soon as the foliage yellows and dies back. It's important to clean out the dying leaves—but only once they've

POPPY SPECIES

Of the four main contributors to the spectacle of color in the late-spring garden, two are European annuals: *Papaver somniferum*, the breadseed or opium poppy (which is sometimes rumored to be illegal, but is in fact legal to grow for garden use in the United States), and *P. rhoeas*, the corn, Shirley, or Flanders poppy. *P. nudicaule*, the Icelandic poppy, is a delicate perennial best treated as an annual. And *P. orientale*, the Oriental poppy, is a big, showy perennial, and one to grow if you live in a hotter climate.

The OPIUM POPPY, also known as the breadseed poppy, is a hardy annual that can grow up to 4 feet tall in Zones 7 to 10. We grow a few versions at the farm, as I did at Turkey Hill in Westport. They can produce quite large ornamental seedpods after blooming, which look beautiful in the garden and can be dried for arrangements. I have 'Black Peony', 'Rose Peony', 'Danish Flag', and 'Lauren's Grape', among other varieties, in my gardens.

The CORN POPPY grows from 1 to 3 feet tall, has flowers of about 3 inches in diameter, and is hardy from Zones 4 to 8. In its wild form, *P. rhoeas* is pure scarlet, but hybridization has greatly enlarged the color range. The 'American Legion' variety is bright red. One strain, the Shirley poppy, bred by a Reverend W. Wilks in Shirley, England, in the late nineteenth century, bears flowers in pastel shades banded in white. Hybridized strains such as 'Fairy Wings' offer glowing purples and shades of slate and mauve tinged with gray.

The ICELANDIC POPPY comes in more than eighty varieties, grows 1 to 2 feet tall, and blooms from late spring through summer; it can also rebloom, as it does in Katonah, in very late summer or early fall, as the weather cools. Flowers can be orange, red, yellow, apricot, pink, salmon, or white, and the plant is hardy in Zones 2 to 8. It grows well in borders where the slender stems can intertwine with other plants. It also attracts birds, butterflies, and bees; the varieties on my farm tend to self-seed readily and are great bloomers.

The ORIENTAL POPPY blooms from late spring to midsummer for only a few weeks (up to three if it's not too rainy). It comes in brilliant shades, most notably red-orange or bright scarlet with purple-black centers. It can grow up to 4 feet tall and its blossoms can be more than 6 inches in diameter. It has nice leaves in spring and early summer, which die down during the heat but come up again in the fall. It is hardy in Zones 3 to 8. Though I grow many types, the Oriental poppies are some of my favorites—we have them in the cutting garden as well as along the pergola at Katonah.

The easiest and most successful way to show off a bunch of fresh-cut poppies is to place them individually, as we did here with vintage cordial glasses arranged on a cut-glass tray. With stems clipped short, the naturally floppy poppy will stand upright in a small vessel. This tableau spotlights several varieties from my garden (clockwise from bottom left): red 'Drama Queen', lavender 'French Flounce', rosy red 'Oh La La', classic red-orange Oriental poppies, 'Lauren's Grape', pinkish purple 'Cupcake', and frilly 'Sugar Plum'.

turned brown or black and are fully past. Unless you are saving the seeds (or waiting for decorative seed heads), deadhead the plants immediately after flowering to encourage more blooms before the end of the season.

PROPAGATING Poppies self-seed heavily, so what begins with one flower can easily turn into many. You can also propagate Oriental poppies with root cuttings. When the plants are dormant, dig up a clump of poppies, cut the "mother plant" clump midway down its roots, and separate the new root clump into individual pieces. Plant cuttings in potting mix and plant the emerging seedlings in the garden in spring.

TROUBLESHOOTING Poppies rarely attract pests or insects (other than beneficial ones like bees), but they can be prone to fungal diseases or rot in wet soil or damp weather conditions. If you know your garden is prone to damp conditions and diseases such as mildew or leaf spot, use an all-purpose fungicide preventively, and always discard—do not compost—any diseased foliage.

HOW TO ARRANGE

CUTTING Corn poppies and Icelandic poppies are varieties that make especially good cut flowers. Cut the blooms when the buds are standing upright and show a bit of color—just before the petals are ready to open out. When cutting poppies, keep a bucket of water at your side so that you can plunge the stems directly into it. If there's severe weather in the forecast, cut any blooming poppies sooner rather than later. A heavy rainfall can decimate the delicate petal structure, leaving your flowers denuded and crushed; likewise, a sudden early-season heat wave can "cook" the blooms right off your poppies (mature plants, later in the summer, should be able to withstand a little heat).

MAINTAINING With poppies and other flowers that have a milky sap in the stem (such as hollyhocks), it's very important to seal the cut end, or they will wilt quickly in arrangements. Use a match, a candle, or a gas flame to singe the end of the stem, or dip it in boiling water for twenty to thirty seconds. This stops the flow of sap, which can clog the stem and prevent it from taking in water. After singeing, place the flowers in fresh water.

ARRANGING Poppies have a tendency to flop; you can prop them up by setting them next to sturdier flowers that can act as supports. With their concentration of color and their dark centers, putting them at the heart of an arrangement draws the eye in and gives the grouping a layered depth.

The vibrant reds of Orientals are a perfect companion to green accents, such as a fern or the dark, variegated and pointed leaf of the Virginia knotweed (*Persicaria virginianum*). The mimosa tree is particularly fragrant when poppies are in bloom, and its sunny yellow flowers on swooping branches are among Kevin's favorites (see page 166). Poppies are beautiful even when they've dropped their petals—the dried seedpods make great sculptural elements within a bouquet.

Poppy petals can be extremely fragile, so arranging with these flowers is a lesson in patience. Take care when positioning a bloom or manipulating an arrangement; plan ahead to avoid handling the delicate flower heads too much. Icelandic poppies are more long lasting and stable in arrangements than Oriental varieties. You can show off their twisting, turning stems and ruffled petals in an airy display. (To stand the stems upright, use a spiked frog in the bottom of the vase.)

The addition of the beautiful green *Gunnera* leaf took this mix of opium poppy hybrids (including 'Lauren's Grape', 'Drama Queen', 'Cupcake', and 'Raspberry Breadseed') and lady's mantle in a delightfully unexpected direction. "This is the arrangement that changed my life when it came to arranging flowers," says Kevin. "Martha was putting in tons of poppies and adding the lady's mantle—and to me, it looked beautiful and finished." But it needed one more thing—a big green leaf. As he puts it, "So I hand her this *Gunnera* leaf, and she sticks it into the side—and suddenly it went from being this balanced arrangement that's easily understood to becoming a masterpiece that you could just sit and stare at all day."

In this arrangement,
your eye is immediately
drawn to the poppy,
with its focus-stealing
bright red petals and
dark center. With a star
flower like this one,
add supporting players
within a limited palette
of two or three colors.
White-species peonies
and tufts of light-green
lady's mantle give the
bouquet body, slender-
budded *Baptisia* stems
extend its reach, and
striated *Carex* grasses
flow over the edges of
the pitcher, mimicking
the branches of the
trees in the English
transferware pitcher's
Blue Willow pattern.

An intricately patterned Edwardian-era bone-china pitcher with a gold vermeil glaze has a wide mouth that encourages a mass of flowers. Here, that flower is the iconic poppy, the red Oriental, with its deep, dark center. It's combined with orange Oriental lilies in bud and bloom to create a lush portrait in warm, saturated color. To break up all that red, Kevin added green leaves—spotted *Pulmonaria* (lungwort) and striped *Oxalis* (wood sorrel).

The blooms of double-peony-flowered 'French Flounce' poppies are dense, textured, gorgeous tufts. By design, this arrangement—composed as a pair, in shiny wire woven vases atop a silver tray—mimics the shape of the blossom itself. The ruffled leaves of lady's mantle (*Alchemilla*) mirror the poppies and anchor them, while lady's mantle flowers lend frothy grace notes.

OPPOSITE: A cream-ware bowl is the natural choice for a vessel meant to hold a profusion of blooms in creamy shades. Here, Kevin took a palette of pastels inspired by his favorite candies to create an arrangement that gathers three of the most joyful signs of spring and summer: poppies, fragrant mimosa, and tulips. The structure of the Icelandic poppy stem makes it easier to work with than the floppy Oriental, but a cage frog placed inside will allow you to precisely manipulate the flowers.

For a fragrant bouquet that shows off the range of clematis colors, Kevin picked four varieties from the pergola at Katonah. The deeply saturated purple of 'Rhapsody' anchors the center, while lavender 'Eyre's Gift', pale lavender 'Blue Angel', and white 'Snow Queen' surround it in a glass trophy-shaped vase. Smaller white rambling roses in full bloom and feathery Japanese painted ferns lighten the arrangement; the ferns also play on the clematis color palette.

Clematis

CLEMATIS

I FIRST FELL IN LOVE WITH CLEMATIS WHEN I PLANTED MY GARDENS AT TURKEY HILL. AT THAT TIME, I REALLY DID NOT FOCUS ON THE LARGE-FLOWERED TYPES—THE 'NELLY MOSER', C. JACKMANII, AND 'MRS CHOLMONDELEY'— BUT RATHER ON THE FRAGRANT SPRING BLOOMERS: C. MONTANA AND C. VIRGINIANA, PLANTED AT THE BASE OF WALLS AND PILLARED SHADE TERRACES.

They grew very well, covering great areas with pink and white star-like flowers. I even had the scent collected for future use as a perfume because it was so delightful.

Years later, when I was planning the design of the landscape at the farm in Katonah, one very important feature on the list of "requirements" was a clematis pergola. I had visited a master clematis grower in California and fallen in love with blue and lavender and purple varieties, and I was determined to somehow grow these beautiful vines in all my favorite colors. I conferred with the growers, and they assured me they could provide many different plants in a variety of "blues." The bower or trellis supports were sixty-two Chinese granite grape stakes, and to make it easier for the vines to climb, I wound copper wire around each of the 8-foot-tall uprights. This has

Because they have such short stems on the vine, clematis blossoms are tailor-made for floating arrangements. This simple, elegant grouping of white clematis and purple and white passion flower includes the plant's own greenery, taking its cues from the flower's natural growing pattern. Here, the shape of each bowl echoes the symmetry of the flower petals, while the foliage and stems decorate the area outside the vessels, creating an especially pretty centerpiece on a lavender linen runner.

worked extremely well and the vines, now more than ten years old, reach all the way to the top of the stakes every year.

Clematis are easy to grow, but they are also prone to some very serious diseases, which cause the entire vine to wilt and dry up. This happened one year and I thought I had lost the entire grouping; but after being hacked to the ground, the vines re-emerged better than ever. The pergola has been a focal point, the clematis underplanted with blue catmints (*Nepeta* x *faassenii* and *N. racemosa* 'Walker's Low'), orange poppies, and hundreds of several types of purple allium. Not only does the border look good for months, it serves as a great source for cut flowers and "catnip" for my beautiful cats.

I first saw clematis used in bouquets and arrangements in California. Graceful and arching, the vines lend themselves to loose, ethereal arrangements, and the white varieties are very effective in wedding bouquets, too. I am now rethinking my hesitation to have other colors of clematis in the gardens and have planted the massive white varieties in my small garden of all white flowers—they grow nicely on pyramidal *tuteurs*. I have also started planting the vines on other walls and at the bases of trees. Because there are only about three hundred species of clematis, it is not too large a genus to get to know well. And the rewards both inside and out are immeasurable.

GROWING
& ARRANGING

*KNOWN AS THE QUEEN OF THE CLIMBERS, CLEMATIS
PLANTS ARE EXTREMELY ADAPTABLE, AND WILL GLADLY
HOOK ONTO AND TRAVEL UP TRELLISES, FENCES,
ARCHES, OR TREES. THOUGH THEY'RE NOT AS WIDELY USED
AS CUT FLOWERS, THEY MAKE STRIKING ARRANGEMENTS.*

HOW TO GROW

Clematis is a genus of about 300 species within the buttercup family *Ranunculaceae.* The distinctive blooms are widely known as clematis, but have also been called traveller's joy, virgin's bower, old man's beard, leather flower, and vase vine. With the right care, clematis can climb structures more than 20 feet tall. Their tendrils twist and curl because the touch of a stake or branch stimulates growth on the opposite side of the stem. The blooms appear all summer long, making them a true garden great.

ZONE Clematis generally grows best in Zones 3 to 9, depending on the cultivar. They are generally hardy, and some varieties can even succeed in the varied winter temperatures of Zone 10. 'Comtesse de Bouchaud' and 'Duchess of Edinburgh' can handle even regions as far south as Florida.

SOIL Clematis need moist, well-drained soil that's neutral to slightly alkaline. Amend the planting hole with compost, and make sure the surface stays moist and cool.

LIGHT Make sure these climbers have access to at least five hours of sun each day. Some varieties will bloom in partial shade, however, and the plant roots should be shaded to keep them cool and moist. This can be accomplished using low-growing plants or 2 to 3 inches of mulch.

CHOOSING If you buy clematis as a container-grown plant, condition the root-ball, pot and all, by letting it sit in shallow water for twenty to thirty minutes before planting. If buying a tall plant, stake it immediately. Purchase shorter vines in early spring or late autumn.

PLANTING Select a site that will give the foliage and flowers full sun but will also supply a cool, moist place for the root run. Underplanting helps—at the farm we plant catmint and grape hyacinth. Plant deeply—the crown should be at least 2 inches below the surface of the soil. Make sure to build any climbing structures before the roots go in.

It's the nature of the clematis vine to climb, typically 6 to 10 feet (although some grow as tall as 20 feet). Thus, it's important to provide the plants with a structure that it can attach itself to—whether natural or man-made. Most clematis are lightweight vines that can grow atop or through other garden plants without any adverse effects. On the farm in Katonah, clematis bloom not only up and around the pergola (see next page), but also along tree trunks throughout the property (see right). To encourage clematis to keep climbing, use soft, flexible twine to give the vines some extra support and train them to climb in the direction you prefer.

WATERING & FERTILIZING Clematis should be watered about an inch or so weekly, more deeply during dry spells. Cut back water in rainy

Even without a pergola or other dedicated structure, clematis vines should grow vertically without any trouble. Here, in an area separate from the blooming pergola, 'Arabella' clematis finds purchase on the bald cypress tree, which also offers a cool environment for the shade-loving roots.

years to prevent fungus. Feed with superphosphate in autumn and with a balanced organic fertilizer during bud and after bloom.

PRUNING In late fall or early winter, cut back most of your clematis plants to about 4 to 6 inches from the ground to encourage a bushier, stronger growth. Give more delicate or older varieties a gentler pruning.

Depending on the cultivar, clematis bloom differently and need specific pruning strategies. Spring-blooming varieties flower on side shoots of the old season's stems, while summer and fall bloomers flower on new stems. Prune spring-flowering vines immediately after the last flowers have dropped, and do not cut back more than a third of the stems. For summer-flowering varieties, wait until early spring, a few months before flowering, to prune; remove dead or weakened stems and lop off stems above the first large, swollen buds. Clematis stems are delicate, so handle with care when pruning and training the direction of growth. Use narrow-bladed pruning shears and move gently.

TROUBLESHOOTING Keep your eye out for clematis wilt, a fungus that turns stems and flowers black and brown (this is more likely to occur with large flowering varieties than small). To treat, cut off wilting stems just below the infection, and never compost diseased vines. If powdery mildew is a problem, spray lightly with an organic fungicide.

HOW TO ARRANGE

CUTTING Clematis is often overlooked as an arrangement flower, but there are myriad suitable varieties; I grow as many as I can. Some can be slightly more challenging; the woody vines wrap and tangle around each other, so be sure to extract the stems with care. They break very easily and require patience and a tender hand, but they're worth it. When going for a whole vine with clippers, try to untangle the branches while they're still on the plant, to avoid cutting away more than you intended—or the wrong stem of blooms entirely.

ARRANGING The large-flowering varieties work best for a simple arrangement: Cut three and arrange them in small vases, bowls, or other vessels down the length of the table. This allows for an up-close appreciation of the flower's shape and color. Or mix them with hostas or other large leaves in a bubble bowl. Because clematis grow on a vine, they can offer the benefit of movement to an arrangement in a way that is unlike any other flower. Always embrace the curves of their unpredictable stems—the trailing vines can elongate a bushy arrangement or add an unexpected element to a domed bouquet.

CLEMATIS VARIETIES

I have always loved these flowering vines and over the years, I have grown many varieties. Here are a few currently grown in Katonah:

'**RHAPSODY**' has creamy-yellow stamens amid 4- to 5-inch sapphire blue flowers.

'**PARISIENNE**' has large flowers that are light violet-blue with overlapping petals. They appear extravagantly in early summer and then repeat later in the season.

'**BLUE ANGEL**' is a large-flowered variety with 4- to 6-inch blooms. The flowers have ruffled edges and yellow-green stamens.

'**ARABELLA**' is a prolific bloomer.

'**BLUE RAVINE**' boasts brilliantly colored, soft violet blooms with leathery-textured foliage.

'**BETTY CORNING**', first discovered growing in Albany, New York, in 1932, has slightly fragrant, bell-shaped flowers that bloom from summer to fall. It typically grows to 6 feet tall and features single, nodding, pale lilac flowers with recurved tips.

The sweet autumn clematis, *C. terniflora,* is a swift, easy, and highly adaptable ground cover, creating a drift of snow in early September when its fragrant, creamy white flowers appear.

The long pergola (top) stands along the carriage road leading up to my home in Katonah. Varieties include pale 'Blue Angel' (bottom left), star-shaped and striated 'Parisienne', and deep blue 'Rhapsody' (bottom right).

Transparent trumpet vases give tender clematis vines structure, allowing these flowers to do what comes naturally to great effect. 'Eyre's Gift' clematis in three stages of growth, with its sharp edges and star-shaped petals, counters the soft, ruffly effect of Kevin's favorite cream-colored peonies. Leaving foliage on both stems adds to the direction of the grouping, which reaches above as it gestures gracefully below. This is a good example of matching stems to vase to accentuate the form of both. *OPPOSITE:* Large star-shaped blooms and tiny bell-shaped flowers; petals in bright white, deep purple, pale lavender, sapphire blue, and scarlet—clematis is a genus with many faces, and I happen to love, and grow, a wide variety of them. Here, several varieties are placed separately in small glass vases and grouped on a silver tray in order to highlight the form of each individual flower.

Play up the long, slender
nature of the delphin-
ium by giving it an
equally tall, slender vessel like these vintage
wine bottles and milk-
glass soda bottles.
Bicolor begonia leaves
accent the ombré
pattern of blues. Here,
Kevin placed a few extra
blossoms that were
trimmed near the bot-
tom of a stem into a
shorter vessel alongside
the shooting spires.

Delphinium

DELPHINIUM

---

*IT'S ALWAYS INTERESTING FOR A GARDENER LIKE MYSELF
TO COME ACROSS A FLOWER THAT IS ESPECIALLY BEAUTIFUL
YET EXTREMELY DIFFICULT TO GROW. THE DELPHINIUM IS THAT
TYPE. I HAVE BEEN CHALLENGED FOR YEARS TO GROW
THE TOWERING BLUE SPIRES THAT I FIRST SAW AT THE ROYAL
HORTICULTURAL SOCIETY CHELSEA FLOWER SHOW IN LONDON,
AND IN THE INCREDIBLE GARDENS OF FRANK CABOT IN QUEBEC.*

I even got to see such flowers right across from my Turkey Hill garden in Westport
when the proprietor of a flower farm grew some from seeds of English hybrids—they
were as amazing as any I had ever laid eyes on.

I had read about delphinium and its culture in one of my favorite books, *A Wom-
an's Hardy Garden,* by Helena Rutherfurd Ely. She grew incredible flowers in Vernon,
New Jersey, on her sprawling estate with the help of scores of accomplished gardeners.
She warned that the plants were prone to mildew and insects, and cautioned unsus-
pecting readers that a dusting of wood ash from the fireplace was a good antidote. So
I did everything she advised and actually, in my Middlefield garden in the Berkshire
Mountains, did succeed in propagating and growing some respectable, if-not-8-feet-tall,

"OF COURSE, THERE ARE
NOW EXTRAORDINARY PINKS AND
CREAMS AND LAVENDERS, BUT
I STILL MELT WHEN I OBSERVE A
3-FOOT STALK OF ELECTRIC-BLUE
DELPHINIUMS."

spires of Pacific Giant hybrids. The nights of Massachusetts were still cool back then, in the 1960s and '70s, and everything in my small gardens there grew extremely well.

Katonah is often too warm after May to grow beautiful flower spikes, and so is East Hampton. But Maine is exactly right—I grow not only delphinium like Mr. Cabot but also another hard-to-grow flower, *Meconopsis*, or Himalayan blue poppy, like he did at Les Quatre Vents, near the mouth of the St. Lawrence River.

He was an exemplary gardener and garden visionary, and I was lucky enough to meet him and talk with him about his ability to make Mother Nature do what he wanted her to do. His best advice: Plant what you want in as ideal an area as history or another gardener tells us. Choose showy plants that delight and astound—the blue poppy, the chanterelle mushroom, giant *Astilboides tabularis*, *Corydalis flexuosa* 'China Blue', *Podophyllum peltatum* (mayapple)—and plant them in massive quantities where they can be viewed from a good vantage point. Make walks nearby the great plantings so viewing will be seemingly "accidental but intended."

His delphiniums were carefully placed in a sunny border where winds were staved off by a great stand of tall trees. If there were stakes supporting the spires, they were so carefully placed as to be almost invisible. And the delphiniums were more often than not the showy blue colors that we so admire and love. Of course, there are now extraordinary pinks and creams and lavenders, but I still melt when I observe a 3-foot stalk of electric-blue flowers.

I am growing nice delphiniums in my Maine garden, and Kevin and I cut them to desired lengths for arranging in the beginning of August when most of the flowers along the stems have opened. They look nice in tall slender vases, but I still prefer them, en masse, in a mixture of shades. There are now New Zealand–bred hybrids (*Delphinium* x *elatum*, the Elatum group) that have strong stems and vigorous growth and are truly perennial. Try some of those. And good luck!

Although delphiniums look spectacular on their own, they can also add personality to a mixed arrangement of early-summer beauties. Kevin used an antique Japanese cast-iron brazier designed to resemble bamboo as an anchor for this display. He started with a floral frog, placing a cloud of hydrangea around the base, then inserted dianthus, poppies, and hollyhocks (in bud and bloom), which extended the lavender palette, and a spire of 'Dusky Maiden' delphinium, which elevates the grouping.

DELPHINIUM 181

GROWING
& ARRANGING

*GLAMOROUS AND ARISTOCRATIC DELPHINIUM SPIRES COME IN
COLORS NOT OFTEN SEEN ELSEWHERE IN THE GARDEN—
MOST NOTABLY BLUES, INCLUDING ULTRAMARINE, CELESTIAL,
AND IRIDESCENT EXAMPLES. THESE SPECTACULAR TALL
BLOOMS THRIVE IN COOL CLIMATES AS LONG AS THEY GET
PLENTY OF SUN AND CONSIDERABLE CARE.*

HOW TO GROW

Delphiniums can be a challenge to cultivate. Though listed in the perennial books, most are only truly perennial in their ideal climate, and are generally short-lived. With lots of sunshine and cool, moist summers, however, delphiniums can grow to staggering heights.

There are a few species groups of delphiniums. The Belladonna group includes blue or white flowers that grow 3 to 4 feet tall. You'll find taller plants (3 to 8 feet) and more colors in the Elatum group. English hybrids reach upward of 8 feet high and boast individual double florets 3 to 4 inches in diameter. Their colors range from the rarest true blue to lilac, mauve, purple, pink, and white, with centers (called bees) that may be black, brown, fawn, white, or even striped. The Pacific Giant hybrids, developed in California by Frank Reinelt in the 1930s and '40s, have become the industry standard, with spikes up to 9 feet tall. Originally bred to behave like annuals, they are now grown from seed-started plants.

ZONE Areas with cool, moist summers—Maine, Alaska, Oregon, or, better yet, coastal Canada— are the delphinium's preferred places to grow. Winter is not a problem for most delphiniums. The species we grow, including the most popular strains of hybrids, are hardy to Zone 3, meaning they can survive wintertime lows as extreme as 30 degrees below zero.

It's the heat and lack of moisture that they object to—they grow best to Zone 7.

SOIL Well-drained, fertile soil with a pH that is neutral to slightly alkaline is key to success with delphiniums. When planting, prepare soil 1 foot deep with organic matter. Then use balanced fertilizer (such as 10:10:10) and a healthy mulching with rich compost to keep the roots moist. Reapply fertilizer and compost after the first blooms have been cut back (leave the foliage to grow until the later-season flower shoots begin to appear). They are heavy feeders, so add composted manure every autumn.

LIGHT Delphinium heads require full sun—six to eight hours a day—to thrive, while their roots need cool, moist shade.

CHOOSING Because delphiniums act more like biennials in many zones, gardeners must start fresh each year with new plants, which can be grown from seed or purchased in pots. Planting from seed requires patience (often yielding only foliage the first year and not flowering until the second), but is the easiest method for growing these tricky blooms. If you want a full row of beautiful blue spires, as I have in the cutting garden in Maine, buy or propagate plenty extra. If you're buying delphinium plants from a nursery, look for healthy plants in bud. Avoid plants that have

There are very few true blue flowers in nature, so *Delphinium* 'Cobalt Dreams' stands out. Let the qualities that make the flower special in the garden—its height, color, and variety on the stem—be your guiding principles once you bring it inside, with arrangements that play to those strengths.

any sign of powdery mildew, fungus, insects, or yellow leaves. Don't buy a plant that has roots running from the bottom of the pot, which indicates it has been in the pot too long and become root-bound, or pot-bound. It won't transplant well.

PLANTING Pick a spot in the garden that is protected from the wind. These tall plants are prone to getting blown over. Dig a hole for the delphinium plant that is about 1 foot deep and twice the diameter of the container. Make sure that the top of the root-ball is level with the soil when planted. Delphiniums should be spaced 1 to 3 feet apart.

As the plants mature, all but the lowest-growing kinds (such as the dwarf forms) will require careful staking to prevent their hollow stems from snapping in the wind or rain. Stake the plants when the flower spikes are about a foot tall and continue to stake them as they grow even taller. Tie the plant to the stake at 12- to 18-inch intervals.

WATERING Ample water in the summer is essential. A dried-out delphinium root system can easily kill the plant. The soil should be moist, but without any standing water.

PRUNING Remove faded flower spikes, cutting back to the nearest secondary flower spike. After the plant's first bloom, cut off the spent flower stalk. In the fall, when the bloom is done and the leaves have turned yellow to brown, cut the entire plant down to about an inch from the ground.

PROPAGATING You can propagate by seed, cuttings, or division. To propagate by seed, collect fresh seeds in the fall, allow to dry, and store in an airtight container. Sow indoors in midwinter in a tray or pot with vermiculite or another seed starter. The seeds do best in a cooler place (60 to 68 degrees); keep them moist and they will typically germinate in two to four weeks.

To use cuttings, take 4-inch basal cuttings in the spring. The cutting should be solid (not hollow) and the center of the stem should be white. From the side, cut shoots coming out of the plant's crown, not the hollow flowering stems. Root the cutting in part shade in sand or in a sand-peat mix.

To propagate by division, divide plants carefully in the spring every four or five years, ensuring each divided section contains three or more shoots, and replant immediately.

TROUBLESHOOTING There's a forbidding list of pests and diseases that target delphinium, from slugs and snails to tiny cyclamen mites, and fungal outbreaks such as powdery mildew, leaf spot, and crown rot, some of which are brought on by summer temperatures and humidity. Fight them with organic fungicide and neem oil. Keep your eye on the plant's crown, which is susceptible to problems. If the plant becomes heavily diseased, remove it completely, before it can infect surrounding plants. A word of caution: Delphinium seeds and plants (especially when young) are toxic if eaten; keep them away from children, pets, and grazing animals.

HOW TO ARRANGE

CUTTING Wait until many flowers are open before cutting delphinium spires. That said, you can include buds in arrangements; several stems can add variety. Cut the stems at a 45-degree angle so as much water can be absorbed as possible, and then place them in a bucket of lukewarm or cold water. Delphinium foliage isn't attractive—it's dense and breaks easily—so it's best to remove it, especially any that will be underwater in the vase. Prepping these flowers is important, as the stems tend to deteriorate. Clean them well before putting them in the vase.

MAINTAINING Hollow stems need to stay full of water. Recondition delphiniums every two to three days by recutting the stems and changing the water. Keep flowers in a cool area out of direct sunlight.

ARRANGING Delphiniums are very beautiful arranged alone or en masse—they don't necessarily need other flowers to join in. So let the dramatic flowers stand strong as a single stem in a narrow cylinder. Or mass them in a wide-mouthed vase, using the same color palette; crisscross their stems for balance. They are surprisingly light, so although you may worry that a delphinium arrangement will be top-heavy, simply use a vase with a solid base and let the flowers soar.

This towering bouquet of delphiniums is built around the same color palette. Its flowers are in all stages of bloom along each stem, which are held together in a sizeable flip glass. The "flip" was used back in the eighteenth and early nineteenth centuries to drink heated spiced liquor mixed with beaten eggs. Today its flared rim is ideal for flowers.

Hydrangea

HYDRANGEA

I'VE GROWN HYDRANGEAS HAPHAZARDLY FOR MANY YEARS. I PLANTED MY FIRST SHRUBS IN EAST HAMPTON ABOUT TWENTY-FIVE YEARS AGO. THERE WAS A LONG BORDER ON THE EAST SIDE OF THE ONE-ACRE PLOT THAT NEEDED FILLER UNDER GIANT RHODODENDRONS AND VIBURNUMS, AND SINCE HYDRANGEAS ARE AN IMPORTANT PLANT IN THE HAMPTONS, I BOUGHT A FEW VARIETIES OF MIXED TYPES AND COLORS.

They grew extremely well and fit into the landscape plan very nicely. When I redid that garden a few years ago, I planted only various white hydrangeas throughout, replacing my beloved roses with a different kind of blooming plant (and moving the colored hydrangeas to Katonah). We planted 'Incrediball' shrubs, *H. paniculata* trees, climbing hydrangea (*H. petiolaris*), many *H. macrophylla*, 'Anabelle' (*H. arborescens*), lacecap 'Windermere', and *H. paniculata* 'Grandiflora'. I had specifically planned for strong-stemmed flowers and large-growing shrubs. I have not been disappointed in the least—every shrub has prospered and produced masses of great blooms. All the hydrangeas from East Hampton transplanted very well to Katonah, and I have started a large curved garden on the edges of the Maple Woodland, which is growing well.

"I HAD PLANNED FOR STRONG-STEMMED FLOWERS AND LARGE-GROWING SHRUBS. I HAVE NOT BEEN DISAPPOINTED IN THE LEAST—EVERY SHRUB HAS PRODUCED MASSES OF GREAT BLOOMS."

I am enjoying the process of starting lots of hydrangeas from cuttings of unusual types and colors that I receive in bouquets from florists. Hydrangeas are very easy to propagate—within three to four years, a shrub grown from a cutting should bloom in the garden. This kind of propagation can be achieved in sand, using a rooting hormone to stimulate growth.

My friend Dan Hinkley travels the world looking for undiscovered species of plants, and he has brought back some lovely delicate flowering hydrangeas in varying shades of mauve and purple from Asia. Dan offers great advice for growing this wonderful shrub: He prefers planting in partial shade, under a high canopy of deciduous trees, feeding heavily once a year. He also suggests growing several different types of this practical plant—oakleaf (*quercifolia*), mophead (*macrophylla*), and lacecap hydrangea.

Frank Cabot adapted climbing hydrangeas to his landscape, planting these useful plants at the base of his tallest trees. His forest looks amazing, with the trunks of his trees emblazoned with white flowers protruding from healthy climbing hydrangeas. I have followed his lead and have done this on many trees throughout my garden. The vines enhance the trees, and the trees look so good enshrouded in white flowers.

Hydrangea macrophylla is a showy bigleaf variety that is excellent in all its possible habitats: on the bush in the garden, cut in arrangements, and left to preserve its blossom in dried form. The name comes from the Greek makros, meaning "large," and phyllon, meaning "leaf."

Most hydrangeas are very good cut flowers. A single mophead in a water glass can turn heads if the flower is oversize, and a great bouquet of *paniculata*, the way my friend Harry Slatkin displays them, is long lasting and incredibly impactful in a big room.

I sometimes pick just one of each and every type of blue hydrangea in the garden, stick them in small water glasses, and line them up down the center of the breakfast table—how beautiful and informative. (I do this with many of my flowers if I have a good quantity of different types.) And Kevin likes to mix hydrangeas with other flowers for contrast—this results in very successful and beautiful bouquets (as you can see on the following pages).

GROWING
& ARRANGING

*HYDRANGEAS BOAST SHOWY, OLD-FASHIONED APPEAL
AND WILL FLOURISH IN ALMOST ANY GARDEN. EASY
TO CARE FOR, A SHRUB CAN PRODUCE A PROFUSION OF
FOLIAGE AND THE MOST VOLUPTUOUS BLOSSOMS.*

HOW TO GROW

Hydrangeas are easygoing shrubs that adapt to a variety of soils. They'll thrive with regular water and at least partial sun. Just make sure to prune according to the variety you're growing (see Pruning, page 194). The result should be big, beautiful blooms.

ZONE Some hydrangea varieties such as the panicle (*paniculata*) are cool-hardy and can be planted from Zones 3a to 8. Old-growth plants including *macrophylla* (bigleaf) and *quercifolia* (oakleaf) can live in climates as cold as Zone 5b. Smooth hydrangea (*arborescens*) is hardy to Zone 4a.

SOIL While these plants can thrive in nearly any moist, well-drained soil, a soil's pH level may influence the color of the flowers in the bigleaf group. Acidic soils (pH zero to 7) tend to deepen blue shades, while alkaline environments (pH 7 to 14) brighten pinks and reds. To test the pH of your soil, use a simple kit (available at any nursery). For a more accurate reading, consult your regional extension agency for information on professional soil testing. You can also adjust the soil's pH at the time of planting—something you might consider if your soil is naturally close to 7, as the neutral levels can sometimes cause muddy purple-hued blossoms. Increase the acidity and encourage blue flowers by adding sulfur (something we do at the farm in Katonah) or a sulfur-based mix called Hydrangea Blueing, available at nurseries. To increase the alkalinity instead, add lime. Blue tends to be the more popular choice, but the pinks and reds can be unusual and lovely. Skip some of the alternative theories you may have heard, like adding pennies to the soil—these remedies don't always work, and using the proper supplements should yield better, more reliable results.

LIGHT Shrubs will tolerate partial or half shade, but they prefer full sun in cooler climates, especially near the coast. Filtered sunlight is always better for the large leaves, which tend to wilt in bright, midday light. In insufficient light, hydrangeas will become lanky and produce fewer blossoms; they might also be susceptible to powdery mildew.

CHOOSING Most hydrangea plants can be purchased bare-root or in containers (my preference). They should be compact and not blooming, if possible. Inspect plants for signs of wilting leaves or distorted growth patterns, and make sure the plant is not root-bound (see page 184).

PLANTING The best time to plant hydrangeas is in spring or fall. Enrich the soil with equal parts compost and aged manure, plus a handful of all-purpose fertilizer. Dig a hole that will accommodate the root-ball and make

Here, a mix of varieties, including 'Nikko Blue', show their late-summer blooms in a photograph from my Lily Pond home in East Hampton. I've since repainted the trim on the house, from teal to tan. In 2014, some of these shrubs were transplanted to Katonah, where they continue to thrive, but there are still plenty of hydrangeas at Lily Pond.

BIGLEAF, *PANICULATA*, OAKLEAF, AND CLIMBING HYDRANGEAS

Three especially easy-to-grow hydrangeas good for cutting and drying are the bigleaf, the *paniculata* (or panicle), and the oakleaf.

BIGLEAF OR MOPHEAD (*macrophylla*) is called *hortensia* in Europe, where it was named after Hortense de Beauharnais, daughter of the French empress Josephine and stepdaughter of Napoleon. An English botanist later obscured the name's origin, assuming that it came from *hortensis,* Latin for "of gardens." Today few are likely to confuse the large, rounded blue, pink, or white heads for anything but the showy bigleaf hydrangea. The species also contains lacecap varieties. Unlike the big, floppy mophead bloom, delicate lacecaps are composed of colorful florets surrounding a lacy cluster of smaller flowers.

H. PANICULATA is a huge, hardy species that may grow 30 feet tall. Its blooms (typically white, pink, or red) are cone-shaped and usually measure 8 to 10 inches long. It was the parent of the popular 'Grandiflora', commonly known as Peegee.

OAKLEAF HYDRANGEA (*H. quercifolia*) was discovered in North America in the 1770s. It has white blossoms and lobed leaves that resemble those of the red oak. This shrub produces a stunning autumnal show as the flowers slowly dry and the leaves turn beautiful shades of russet, yellow, and brown. The flowers, too, can take on a pinkish-red tinge as the weather cools.

CLIMBING HYDRANGEAS (*Hydrangea anomala* subsp. *petiolaris*) are not as common and, though not as useful as cut flowers, they are my favorite kind. They thrive in both shady and sunny conditions, and are hardy in Zones 4 to 8. They flower in late spring and early summer, and show off their exfoliating reddish bark in winter. I love their shiny dark-green foliage and fragrant white flowers. They can grow, unsupported, quite high, climbing even taller mature trees. On my farm, I've planted dozens of them. They climb up the trunks of spruce and sugar maples, up the stone chimneys, and up and over trellises. Avoid letting these vines climb on wooden structures, which can be damaged by the roots.

With an impressive ability to grow 40 to 60 feet high, climbing hydrangea vines (opposite) cling to walls, trellises, and even trees—here, maples and pines just outside the greenhouse in Katonah. 'Glowing Embers' (far right), known as 'Alpenglühen', boasts large clusters of pink blooms, and flowers from summer through fall. It makes a great companion for evergreen shrubs and mass plantings under tall trees. Blooms can change from white to pink to deep purple as they mature throughout the season. I also have lacecaps in Katonah, this one grown from a rare cutting saved from an arrangement (right).

sure it is at least twice its width. Set the plant in the hole and fill with soil. Give extra water only until the transplant takes hold or if the leaves begin to droop. They grow well in clusters and groups; space plants about 3 to 10 feet apart.

WATERING A popular hydrangea myth is that the name comes from their unquenchable thirst for water. In fact, the genus name was formed from the Greek *hydro* (water) and *angeion* (vessel) because the flowers mature into a cup-shaped fruit. Though they do require regular watering, some hydrangeas, including oakleaf and *paniculata,* are fairly drought-tolerant and ideal for gardens where water conservation is considered. The bigleaf varieties require daily watering.

FERTILIZING Work 1½ to 2 inches of compost or composted manure into the soil every year. Add a balanced fertilizer, and mix with sulfur or lime as appropriate for your desired pH level and color output. (For more on color, see Soil, page 190.) On my farm, we also add used coffee grounds weekly—I bring them from the café at my office building in Manhattan. They help add organic matter, as well as acidity—for more of those celebrated "true blue" blossoms.

PRUNING Encouraging blooms is the usual aim of pruning, and knowing the species of a particular variety of hydrangea is the key to success. Generally, the less pruning, the better—so when in doubt, don't prune.

If your hydrangea sets buds on old (the previous season's) wood, including most bigleaf cultivars, prune only when the plants are done flowering, in late winter, and remove only the previous summer's spent flowering stems. Cut out any dead branches along with those that have flowered already, and leave the rest intact. Remontant, or "reblooming," bigleaf cultivars (such as 'Endless Summer', among others) flower on both old and new growth, so no pruning is required. Oakleaf hydrangea varieties also bloom on old wood; remove only dead branches and flowers.

Some species bloom only on new wood, which allows for pruning in late winter or early spring without risk of sacrificing flowers the following summer. These species include *paniculata* and varieties of *arborescens* such as the perennially popular 'Annabelle'.

If you're not sure whether your hydrangea is old wood, think about when it flowers. Old-wood bloomers begin flowering in early summer and are often done by midsummer. On these plants, next year's flower buds form in late summer or early fall.

ABOVE: Kevin prepares to insert a giant *Astilboides* leaf into a grand-scale arrangement of hydrangea (pictured on page 187), playing up the juxtaposition of bloom and foliage. *OPPOSITE:* In the kitchen of my horse stable in Katonah, containers of several varieties of hydrangea are prepared for arranging. After trimming the leaves from the branches, they are returned to their collection containers, which are newly refilled with fresh water. Kevin mixes the different types and sizes of hydrangea among the buckets so as not to crush any of the voluminous flower heads.

PROPAGATING & TRANSPLANTING Hydrangeas are easy to propagate. Cuttings may be taken from a shrub at any stage of maturity, or even from hydrangeas cut for an arrangement. When the cuttings root, they can be planted outdoors. Start with a stem at least 20 inches long, cut it into 4-inch pieces, and remove the leaves. Dip the ends of the cut stems in rooting compound to stimulate root development. Place the stem in a box of water-soaked sand. Mist frequently and keep outside in the shade, where they will root in four to five weeks. To test, pull gently on the top of the stem. If there is resistance, the roots have taken hold; repot plants in individual containers or transplant them to a shady part of the garden. Plant three to five rooted cuttings close together so that the resulting shrub is a hefty size. It takes about three years for cuttings to grow into shrubs large enough to provide cut flowers.

Transplanting hydrangeas is also a simple process that's best accomplished in early spring or late fall, when plants are dormant. For easy transport, prune the hydrangeas to half their size and bag them with a small amount of dirt left around their roots. Dig a hole in the new location and feed with a scoop of organic compost, such as Bio-tone.

TROUBLESHOOTING A hydrangea that won't bloom may have been pruned at the wrong time (see Pruning, page 194). Or it may be losing its buds to cold winters or an unexpected freeze. You can replant it in a sheltered area or wrap it in burlap during chilly months. The hydrangea shrubs in Katonah tend to be problem-resistant; watch for mildew, especially in damp, coastal areas, and treat with fungicide if necessary.

HOW TO ARRANGE

CUTTING Hydrangeas don't cut well when freshly flowering. Wait at least a few weeks after the bloom is completely open, when the blossom has reached its most colorful. The older the bloom, the longer it will last once cut. Cut the flowers in the early morning or late afternoon. To trim stems, use a sharp hand pruner or pocketknife; cut at a diagonal, so that the largest surface area of the stem can be exposed to the water.

MAINTAINING It's essential to properly condition hydrangeas, or they can wilt within hours. Split the ends of the stems to ensure that they will absorb enough water. If the stem is especially woody, use a small hammer to crush the bottom inch or two. Then try this tip: Place the ends of each stem in boiling water for 30 seconds, making sure that the steam does not burn the flower head. Then plunge the cuttings up to the flower head in cold water. Drape damp paper towels across the tops of the blossoms to cover them completely. Mist the paper towels. Do not allow them to dry out. In four hours, your hydrangeas will be fully conditioned.

Remove any leaves that could end up below the water line, since these will rot and encourage the growth of bacteria and algae. Arrange the flowers in fresh water. Keep out of direct light and away from heat sources.

Rehydrate a bouquet of drying cut blooms by floating them in a sink or tub of cold water for three to four hours. Use sharp pruners to recut and resplit the stems to help them draw more water. Refresh the flowers every one to two days, and the arrangement should look fresh for more than a week.

ARRANGING Hydrangea petals are somewhat inconspicuous, but the sepals—the usually unobtrusive leaf-like structures that surround a flower—are bright and showy. And because sepals do not drop off as quickly as petals do, hydrangeas are ideal subjects for long-lasting fresh arrangements. Kevin prefers to design with *paniculata*, which he finds very resilient and easy to work with. They keep their foliage better than *macrophylla*. Often, simpler is better: Let the hydrangeas form a mass of color on their own, or complement the full, rounded shapes of their blossoms with broad hosta leaves.

Bigger vessels are better for these oversize blooms on tall stems, to keep the sense of proportion and to offer support. However, if you cut the stems down, you can use a low, wide vase or bowl. For these arrangements, use chicken wire to secure the stems, as it's easier to manipulate (see page 262).

Late-afternoon light illuminates the breathy blossoms of an all-white hydrangea arrangement with hints of green, mirrored in an Art Deco French painted cast-iron urn. White *H. paniculata*'s dainty sepals make for an airier display than its denser cousins; Kevin removed all foliage to keep the focus on the flowers themselves. He placed young *paniculata* blossoms sparingly throughout the arrangement to create space and lift among the weighty hydrangea blooms. A smaller, breathable bouquet like this one allows for an approachable display that can be placed anywhere.

Arranged in a white ironstone tureen with a flower cage, just a few boughs of 'Blaumeise' hydrangea and wine-colored mophead 'Oregon Pride' form a color-saturated bouquet. The natural shape of the blossom lends itself to a simple dome on short stems.

OPPOSITE: A lofty, large-scale display adorns a Scandinavian table on the second-floor landing in East Hampton. It's composed of the panicle, oakleaf, and mophead hydrangea varieties that line the property; the flowers thrive in coastal areas and they seem to love the rich Long Island soil. Kevin arranged the tall, slender boughs of *paniculata* to appear as if they're jumping from the vase, with denser *macrophylla* as a base. To balance the height and obscure the stems, he tucked 'Autumn Snow' clematis vines into the top of the vessel and draped them around the base.

An arrangement of dense hydrangeas in a pewter compote brings out the colors in a French ticking fabric tablecloth. Use floral putty to secure a cage frog to the bottom of the vessel, then add stems of various heights to stagger the bulbous blossoms and prevent them from crushing one another. Leave some of the hydrangea foliage intact to allow subtle pops of green to peek through the florets. *OPPOSITE:* Kevin arranged green and white mophead and *paniculata* hydrangeas, some with violet edges, in an antique limestone garden urn for a dramatic addition to a grand entryway. Perfect for a formal event, the hydrangeas evoke the richness of Flemish paintings, mingling with broad hosta leaves and cascades of snowberries, jasmine, and amaranth. Though not expensive flowers, either to grow or to purchase, they can nevertheless create a lush, luxurious, and over-the-top arrangement. To assemble, use a ball of chicken wire to hold the stems. Start with the tallest hydrangea blossoms to create fullness and height; insert shorter stems at outer edges and add foliage sparingly on one side. Add graceful vines of jasmine and trailing amaranth around the rim at the end to embrace the asymmetrical arrangement.

Lily

LILIUM

I WAS INTRODUCED TO GARDEN LILIES BY MY FATHER WHEN I WAS ABOUT TEN YEARS OLD. ONE YEAR, HE GREW IMMENSE WHITE LILIES THAT WERE DOTTED WITH DEEP PINK. THE NEXT YEAR, THE NEW LILIES WERE MASSIVE WHITE TRUMPETS THAT HE CALLED EASTER LILIES.

When I was in high school, I entered another of Dad's lilies, which looked a lot like the famous 'Stargazer' (a dotted bright pink blossom with white edges), in a flower-arranging contest held at the Women's Club of Nutley. It was a rather simple arrangement of two lily stalks topped with several huge flowers in a tall, square, silver-luster container. I called it "Fourth of July." I was so happy when it won a blue ribbon, and so was Dad. I encouraged him to plant more lilies. The bulbs were expensive and we were always on a budget, but he splurged for me and bought several each year. They grew very nicely in his garden, getting stronger and taller, so the investment proved worthwhile.

When I planted my first big garden, Turkey Hill, I continued to invest in lily bulbs, planting them throughout my Monet-inspired perennial beds to grow up through the columbines, *Thalictrum*, and the monkshood. I preferred, and still do, the tall upfacing Oriental and trumpet lilies to the Asiatic varieties. But the Aurelians (Asiatic hybrids) and Asiatics have changed drastically in the last couple of decades, and most lilies of all

*"LILIES ARE WONDERFUL FOR
ABOUT TWO MONTHS OF BLOOM,
AFFORDING ME LOTS OF STEMS
FOR GIANT ARRANGEMENTS
OR FOR SMALLER BUD VASES."*

kinds are gorgeous. And now some of the bulb suppliers are shipping amazing examples of Orienpet hybrids, which reach 8 feet in height and are strong, fragrant, and extremely productive. Even the tallest of these lilies needs no staking.

In Maine and Katonah, I grow hundreds of Oriental and Orienpet lilies, and have also discovered the graceful and colorful Turk's cap lilies called Martagons as well as the Japanese *Lilium speciosum*. In some of the older planted areas at Skylands, designed long ago by renowned landscape architect Jens Jensen, the orange Turk's cap lilies grow throughout the laurel and moss, blooming every July and early August. The stalks are tall and graceful, and each has evenly spaced, outward-facing flowers—ten to fourteen per stem. These lilies seed themselves rather easily, it seems, wherever they can find a patch of dirt that has some depth. I have never attempted to transplant these treasures, and I have never seen such lilies offered in catalogs. I just consider myself lucky to have them, and I do what I can to protect them from deer, who love grazing in the woodlands, munching on small trees, flowers, and whatever else they can find.

Deep rich soil and lots of sun are essential elements in growing great lilies. In East Hampton, I grow only 'Casablanca', one of the most beautiful Oriental lilies. The variety was introduced in 1987 by B&D Lilies, and I highly recommend it. The striking outfacing blooms look great in a white garden, and the bulbs thrive year after year. I have successfully transplanted these lilies, after bloom and once the foliage turns brown, and am amazed to see the size that the bulbs attain after four or five years.

I was introduced to a new variety, the Formosa lily, by Dennis Schrader of Landcraft Environments nursery on the North Fork of Long Island. He has fields of these tall self-seeding natives from Taiwan. The lilies are long, white, funnel-shaped trumpets on 4- to 7-foot stems. The flowers are shaded wine-purple on the outer petals, and their scent is absolutely heavenly. They are a must for every flower garden, though once cut, they are not as long-lived as Oriental lilies.

In Maine as well as in Katonah, I plant lots of lilies just for cutting and arranging. Lilies are wonderful for about two months of bloom in the cutting gardens, affording me lots of stems for giant arrangements or for smaller bud vases. In East Hampton, we spend most of our time outdoors and I rarely cut the flowers, preferring to enjoy them while outside, where the scent perfumes the air.

A note of warning: Plant according to directions, digging deep enough and at the correct time of year. I like to plant every bulb in the autumn, permitting them to take hold prior to the freezing of the winter months, although some are shipped only in spring. Remember, also, that planting as soon as the bulbs arrive is a very good habit.

At the entrance to the Summer House in Katonah, a cement faux-bois planter stands sentry. Overflowing with tall white 'Rexona' lilies and asparagus plants (the edible variety, left to open and fern), this arrangement defies all conventions of restraint, reaching sky-high even as it hangs over the top steps. Abundant greenery seems to fill every nook and cranny, while the monochromatic palette gets tiny pops of contrast in the form of the lilies' pollen-rich stamens.

GROWING
& ARRANGING

*DESPITE THEIR ELABORATE APPEARANCE, LILIES ARE
UNFUSSY, WHETHER THE BRILLIANTLY COLORED ASIATIC VARIETY
OR THE GRACEFUL TURK'S CAP. ON THE FARM IN KATONAH
AND AT MY HOME IN MAINE, THESE GORGEOUS, STURDY
FLOWERS HAVE BECOME TRUE STAPLES—OUTSIDE AND INDOORS.*

HOW TO GROW

It doesn't take much to keep lilies happy, but there are a few must-dos. Give them full sun to partial shade (the flowers need sun, but the roots need cool soil). They like well-drained soil that is enriched with organic compost and that is amended a few times a year to keep it that way.

ZONE Lilies require a period of dormancy and cold, so are healthier in the cooler zones of this range. Asiatic lilies grow from Zones 4 to 9, with a few varieties in Zone 10. Martagons (or Turk's cap lilies) are hardy in Zones 3 to 9. Trumpet lilies are best in Zones 5 to 9, and Oriental lilies in Zones 3 to 9.

SOIL Lilies are adaptable to any soil that has been amended with good organic compost and an all-purpose organic fertilizer that's high in phosphorus (the middle number in the indication of nitrogen-phosphorus-potassium; 0:45:0 is one example). Most species and their hybrids respond best to soils that are either neutral or slightly acidic, though a few, including *L. martagon* and *L. regale,* are tolerant of alkaline conditions. They will not thrive in perpetually moist conditions, however, so make sure the soil is very well drained.

LIGHT Lilies love at least six hours of bright sun daily. However, because the roots require cool soil, you can overplant them with ground covers and herbaceous perennials, as we do on the farm, so that the buds and blooms are in full sun but the roots are shaded. More delicate varieties require a bit more shade.

CHOOSING Be sure that bulbs show no sign of rot, such as mushy spots; avoid any with diseased portions. Lily bulbs don't have the same protective layers as those of the tulip, so there may be a higher risk of damage from improper storage. Bulbs should be hydrated and appear rounded (not flat or squashed). Always keep them out of sunlight.

PLANTING Although you can plant lily bulbs in early spring, it's best to plant them in autumn, a couple of weeks before the ground freezes (those planted in spring take a year to catch up). Plant the bulbs immediately, if you can, and keep them out of direct sunlight. As important, plant deep. Lilies need a depth of two to three times the bulb's height. For instance, if the bulb is 2 inches from tip to base, plant no less than 4 inches below the ground level. Their primary feeder roots grow from the underground part of the stem; roots growing from the bulb base are anchors.

A good rule for spacing bulbs is to plant as far apart as the depth you plant. For each lily, dig a relatively large hole, and incorporate organic matter like well-rotted manure or peat moss plus a half cup of high-phosphorus, low-nitrogen fertilizer into the soil.

Lilies, such as the striking pink 'On Stage' variety, add bright color and heady fragrance to the summer garden. They're very adaptable to their surroundings, and are as content in a group as they are in a row. I planted this group of Orienpets surrounded by large plots of lavender and *Ageratum*.

WATERING Plants should be watered regularly, only during the dry season and when in bloom. Focus water at the base and off petals. Make sure that the soil drains well. If water pools in the garden, lilies will rot.

FERTILIZING Lilies are heavy feeders, so give them an organic phosphorus-heavy fertilizer, or top-dress with a tablespoon of tomato fertilizer in springtime when the shoots emerge, and again as they flower.

PRUNING An important (and time-consuming) part of maintaining lilies is to deadhead the spent flowers (but leave the stems). If you don't snip off the dead bloom cluster, it will develop a seedpod, which uses up a lot of the plant's energy that should instead be devoted to fueling the bulb. Once the plant has finished for the season and the stalks are fully brown, cut them down to about an inch from the ground.

TROUBLESHOOTING Lily problems are generally controllable and shouldn't be worrisome. Modern hybrids are resistant but not immune to devastating aphid-borne viruses. Plant tiger lilies (*L. lancifolium*), which are quite prone to viral infections, at least 100 feet from other lilies. If you know your area is at risk for such infections, spray preventively, before there are any signs of disease. Watch for the scarlet lily beetle, which is now found in the Northeast. Be vigilant about handpicking adults and eggs; you can spray larvae—aphids, too—with neem oil, a natural pesticide. Deer love the flavor of lily buds, so spray the plants with an organic repellent.

If a lily display begins to suffer or several stems appear, don't despair; the multiplying bulbs are simply crowded. Carefully dig, separate, and replant after the leaves yellow.

HOW TO ARRANGE

CUTTING Cut the stems so that more than two-thirds of their leaves remain on the plants; after blooming, the foliage produces essential nutrients. Trim stems at a 45-degree angle so the flowers can take in more water. Take care with the pollen from the lily's stamens—it can stain fabrics and irritate skin. If you're planning to arrange with them, it's a good idea to remove the stamens while you're still in the garden: slip on a pair of latex gloves and simply pull off the stamens. That said, if you like the look and texture of them, leave them on—but be aware of nearby clothing or upholstery.

As with tulips, the more stem you leave in the garden, the healthier the plant will be for next year. Kevin prefers to cut long stems for arranging, while I tend to leave more on the plant. Whatever you decide, try not to cut more than half of the total stem length.

MAINTAINING Be sure to strip leaves that would sit below the waterline, and watch for falling stamens. Fill the vase with clean water, and set your arrangement in a cool spot out of direct sunlight. Every couple of days, change the water and retrim the stems. Lilies usually remain fresh for ten days, and sometimes last even longer.

ARRANGING The structure of a stem of lilies is interesting on its own. Avoid crowding lilies in a vase, and experiment with letting just one stem be enough. The Turk's cap lily is brilliant for arranging: its orange petals (covered with maroon spots) curve backward to touch the stem—the graceful shape is the source of the "turk's cap" name.

Lilies can grow very tall (up to 8 feet), so a tall vase is typically in order. At the opposite extreme, you can cut off the blossoms and put them in small bud vases, accompanied by foliage such as a fern frond. Many lilies have multiple colors, so pair them with solid-colored flowers to make the arrangement come together. I like to mix the tubular white trumpets of elegant Asiatic lilies with beautifully spiky verbena. Kevin loves lilies on their own, arranged with some of their leaves or as part of a low-profile centerpiece.

If buying lilies to arrange, choose buds that are just cracking open. If the stems are cut too early, the top buds may not open at all. If the lilies have already bloomed, they will last only a few days. Examine them to ensure that they're in great shape—the petals should not be bruised. Also, keep fragrance in mind when choosing a variety. Some (such as 'Casablanca') are quite overpowering.

Lemony-yellow lilies welcome visitors to the garden behind the Summer House in Katonah. We planted them amid plentiful shrubs so that their extended roots would stay cool in the partial shade the shrubs provide, while their stems and buds get the full sun they need to grow and flower. I stake some of the taller lilies, like 'Gold Sceptre' (bottom left) and 'Silk Road' (bottom right), which can reach 8 feet, with bamboo to keep them upright.

One way to have flowers in the house but maintain the abundance of the garden at the same time is to cut a single lily stem—one that has multiple flowers in bloom as well as buds about to burst. With one stalk you can make small arrangements for an impactful, yet economical display. Let them soar to accentuate the stems, or keep them low with florets. With a flower like *L. auratum* 'Gold Band', which is so singularly beautiful with its 10-inch gold-striped, crimson-spotted blossoms, simply place in a blown-glass decanter. Other varieties include fragrant pink 'Blushing Angel' and the rosy-centered 'Passion Moon', creamy *L. regale*, pendant gold and white 'Mister Cas' in bud and blossom, sunny 'Corcovado', and melon-hued July-blooming 'African Queen'.

An arrangement can be a study in contrasts, of light and dark, of shapes and moods. Here, I combined the white trumpet of tall Formosa lilies with compact *Verbena bonariensis* and the swooping dark "wings" and white trailing tendrils of the bat flower, *Tacca chantrieri,* a beautifully haunting Southeast Asian tropical plant grown in my greenhouse (it also comes in dramatic black). The slender Art Deco vase with its wavy top, mimicking a jack-in-the-pulpit, focuses all eyes on this eccentric assembly of flowers. *OPPOSITE:* A bronze urn in the living room at Skylands holds a massive arrangement of 'Satisfaction' trumpet lilies. Kevin relied on the strong stems (some the width of a quarter) to build a base in a bucket within the urn. Working from the bottom up, start with shorter stems and then add the taller, for a fiery display that shows off the petals from every angle.

Using a cage set into a cement *faux-bois* basket, Kevin created a floral waterfall effect. The papery cups of the annual bells of Ireland (*Moluccella laevis*) grow upright, but when turned and inserted upside down, they create a foam of green spilling over the basket

edge. The distinctive curved and spotted orange blossoms of *L. martagon* are positioned to flow over the bells, and woodland ferns echo the green, but in a more feathery, outward-reaching form. *OPPOSITE:* Lilies easily take center stage in any arrangement, due to

their distinctive shape. With just a dozen blooms of a few varieties from the Katonah garden, arranged in a multichambered vase, they make a strong yet unembellished statement. Varieties include 'Pink Perfection', *L. regale*, 'Stargazer', and 'Gizmo'.

Early Autumn

With our climate in such flux due to global warming and the usual idiosyncrasies of nature, it is rather difficult to plan and plant a garden that will respond to a reliable calendar. Some flowers that we remember blooming only in September in the Northeast now appear as early as August, while others that should bloom in October are in full flower in early September. Nevertheless, if you plan carefully in the spring, you can plant to keep flowers—sunflowers, rudbeckias, bee balm, monkshood, and beautiful dahlias—in view until the first frost.

At the farm, the cooler days of autumn tend to rejuvenate the garden. Many of the plants that were sad and wan come back to life with stronger stems and brighter flowering. The cosmos, snapdragons, and nicotiana produce colorful blooms perfect for autumnal arrangements. The Formosa lilies bloom in September, and they are glorious as we ready the gardens for winter. For me, dahlias are the highlight of the late-flower garden. They come in so many different types, sizes, and colors, and they are easy and wonderful to arrange.

Kevin and I comb through the gardens, looking for plant material that will complement the exotic dahlias and the blooms from the sunflower and rudbeckia

SEASONAL
ALL-STARS

**SUNFLOWER
& RUDBECKIA**

DAHLIA

In late summer and early autumn, there are still plenty of flowers in bloom in the Skylands garden, including sunflowers, rudbeckias, *Gomphrena*, and astilbe. Another advantage of planning our plantings to last the growing season is this final blast of color, just as we are starting to think about putting the garden to bed for the year.

OTHER SEASONAL
HIGHLIGHTS

ASTILBE
QUEEN ANNE'S
LACE
SEDUM
ORNAMENTAL
GRASSES
CHRYSANTHEMUM
KALE
DRIED LEAVES

family. We use fully opened flowers as well as those that are just beginning to open. Vines, seedpods, and fruit on branches such as figs, kiwis, and crab apples make wonderful additions to bouquets. Autumn-blooming clematis, scented geraniums, and grapes can be used as accents in arrangements. And be sure to visit the vegetable garden for late-producing varieties like okra, kale, and cabbages. I remember being entranced by a dinner table decorated with small red cabbages. Savoy cabbages, too, with their crinkly leaves and formidable size, can be extremely effective on buffet tables. Edible vegetables, such as pumpkins, gourds, and squash can be artfully carved to serve as flower containers, or incorporated into arrangements on tables and sideboards.

As winter approaches and your garden is truly laid to rest—cleared of branches and leaves, and top-dressed with manure or compost—think about what you would like in next year's garden and begin the important yet gratifying process of planning. A note of advice, even caution, however, to home gardeners: don't be too eager to clean up your flower beds and put them to sleep. Rather than cutting everything down to the ground, just carefully deadhead and prune. You may be pleasantly surprised by the many plants that keep offering great foliage, seedpods, and dried blooms late in the year. They can look beautiful and colorful in the garden as well as indoors.

LEFT: Working with a warm, golden fall palette, Kevin anchored this arrangement with 'Autumn Joy' sedum, which blooms from August to November and changes in color from pink to copper as it matures. He wove *Gomphocarpus physocarpus* (see page 222) seed heads and dried hydrangea through the sedum and emphasized the color scheme with his choice of a rustic pail to contain the flowers. *RIGHT:* When green has shifted to brown, red, and gold in the garden, make arrangements using branches still bearing fruit, like these persimmon examples. Rust-colored foliage fills in the empty spaces among the branches, and a similarly colored, narrow-necked jar holds everything in place.

Once the blooms are gone from the garden, a display of dried foliage can provide the same punch as a vase full of flowers. Don't overlook the many varieties, color hues, and patterns of the leaves left on plants and in the cutting garden. Here, some leaves are inverted so as to show the striking silver underbelly—the contrast is especially effective when arranged in a ceramic vase with metallic accents, alongside a collection of smaller pewter and silver vessels.

Chrysanthemums are often underrated as an arrangement flower, considered little more than filler for grocery bouquets. But the pop of a ruffled blossom can add warmth and deep color to any setting. Here, the mighty blossoms of golden chrysanthemums are studded with dark cranberry-colored *Heuchera* leaves and placed on a painted tin breakfast tray laden with tea and sugar. The frilliness of chrysanthemums lend themselves to full, dense arrangements, and the petals can stand up to being packed tightly together.

Ornamental kale allows for extended flower production throughout the fall; with creamy white centers accented by a blush of pink, this variety is sometimes known as an ornamental cabbage. For this arrangement, Kevin removed the green outer leaves and paired the richly colored center flowers with lady's mantle and fall leaves from the garden. A set of three smaller arrangements can have the same visual presence as one large display—in this case, without interfering with the artwork above. *OPPOSITE:* One of my favorite plants is *Gomphocarpus physocarpus,* which produces white flowers in summer—but its true usefulness in arrangements comes later, in early autumn, when the large, furry seedpods (or "hairy balls") appear in a vibrant lime green. Here, a single-variety arrangement reflects the green surroundings, the golden edges of the pods playing off the candlesticks. The seedpods are easy to dry and use throughout the fall.

Greens add lightness and movement to a mass of sunflowers (this arrangement includes 'Autumn Beauty', 'Inca Jewels', 'Ring of Fire', and 'Chocolate' varieties) in a weighty, antique brass coal shuttle. Kevin used chicken wire to hold the flowers in place. He then added an explosion of grapevines to draw the eye out, and positioned the lighter flowers toward the bottom of the arrangement to create a layered effect.

Sunflower & Rudbeckia

HELIANTHUS & RUDBECKIA

SUNFLOWERS AND RUDBECKIAS ARE AMONG THE LAST TO BLOOM EACH YEAR. THEY ADD WONDERFUL COLOR IN THE GARDEN AND ALONG FENCES AND WALLS, AND MOST VARIETIES MAKE SUPERB CUTTING FLOWERS.

When my little brother George was planning his wedding at Turkey Hill, both he and Rita, his fiancée, wanted colorful garden flowers as the theme. I suggested planting many types of sunflowers as a backdrop for the luncheon reception tent. By late August, the sunflowers were blooming profusely, and everyone was taking photos of the 10- and 12-foot-tall flowers. On the tables, we were able to arrange asters, rudbeckias, a few dahlias and coleus, and the last of the snapdragons; the effect was charming, homey, and old-fashioned—just what the couple wanted.

Our perception of sunflowers has been of long-stemmed, giant heads, full of black seeds and rimmed with bright yellow petals, swaying in the breeze, nodding to the sun. The fields I first drove past in France and Italy many years ago are still clear in my mind. But now sunflowers come in so many different types and colors. They are no longer cultivated just as a source for seeds and oil, but also for the cut-flower market, where variety is key to their long-standing popularity.

The garden can be as interesting and useful in the autumn as at other times of the

*"THE GARDEN CAN BE AS
INTERESTING AND USEFUL IN
THE AUTUMN AS AT OTHER TIMES
OF THE GROWING SEASON,
THANKS TO MANY VARIETIES OF
SUNFLOWER AND RUDBECKIA."*

growing season, thanks to many varieties of sunflowers and rudbeckias, better known as black-eyed Susans. Mixed into perennial or annual gardens and borders, these will flower late into autumn.

Sunflowers now come in miniature varieties, 2 to 4 feet in height, and others can range from 5 to 10 feet, although I have received photographs from friends and customers of our sunflower seeds depicting plants as tall as 20 feet!

Sunflowers demonstrate a particularly robust character, and that is why I like to plant many along sunny fences, and toward the backs of large gardens. Not only are they perfect for cutting, but when left in the garden they can ripen into food for wild birds. Many sunflowers are annuals, but they often leave seeds, which can grow the following year into healthy plants.

Rudbeckias are vibrant herbaceous perennials, blooming midsummer to late fall if pruned and deadheaded. The flowers last for weeks in the garden. Once largely available only in yellow with dark brown centers, rudbeckias now can be found in many shades of yellow, orange, russet, mahogany, and bronze, with petals arranged in single, semi-double, and fully double rows around dark-centered seed heads. The stems and leaves of rudbeckias are rough and woolly.

The offerings of sunflowers and black-eyed Susans on many roadside farm stands in August and September are outstanding. One can find all sorts of types—the giant seed-centric varieties (great for bird feeders); the more easily used 'Teddy Bear', 'Inca Jewels', and 'Chocolate' sunflowers; and the common black-eyed Susan (*hirtus*) and 'Cherokee Sunset' varieties of rudbeckia.

Kevin mixes these flowers en masse and finds that leafy grapevines, grasses, and even Queen Anne's lace soften and enhance any arrangement of them. I will continue to grow these two types of flowers year after year, and not only will I enjoy the fruits of my labor, but the hungry birds, who are no longer migrating south but hanging around Katonah twelve months a year, will enjoy them even more.

Although they share the same family, Asteraceae, sunflowers and rudbeckias are distinct in their respective genus and species. Rudbeckias have smaller blossoms, although species like *R. laciniata* can grow to 9 feet tall. Rudbeckias have many varieties aside from the commonly known black-eyed Susan, as do sunflowers. Here, the 'Oxeye sunflower' (*Heliopsis helianthoides*) grows at Katonah; known as a "false sunflower," it's actually a perennial sunflower-like member of the same family, and blooms earlier in the season.

GROWING & ARRANGING

BOTH SUNFLOWERS AND RUDBECKIAS EVOKE SUNSHINE IN THE GARDEN. WHILE A WILLOWY RUDBECKIA MAY GROW TO 9 FEET, THERE'S A CERTAIN JACK-AND-THE-BEANSTALK QUALITY TO THE SUNFLOWER. YOU CAN PRACTICALLY WATCH THE STALKS PUSH UP TOWARD THE LIGHT, AS IF THEY WERE HARNASSING SOLAR ENERGY—THEY SOMETIMES GAIN 1 FOOT IN A SINGLE DAY.

HOW TO GROW

Sunflowers and rudbeckias, in all their forms, are in the Asteraceae family, with their signature two sets of florets—the sunny ray florets (the outer petals) and the dark interior disk florets. Growing conditions for each are very similar, with one notable exception: Taller sunflower stalks require staking. Both perennial (*Helianthus*) and annual (*Helianthus annuus*) sunflowers come in hundreds of shapes and sizes, from the giant 'Mammoth Russian' to the dwarf 'Music Box'. And they're fairly easy to grow—as long as they get plenty of sun. The same goes for the approximately twenty species of *Rudbeckia,* whether it's a classic black-eyed Susan (*R. hirta*) or the spiky-petaled *R. subtomentosa.* At Skylands, both grow along the border of the cutting garden; in Katonah, rudbeckias are interspersed throughout the grounds.

ZONE Planted as annuals, sunflowers are hardy in any United States zone. Perennials are hardy from Zones 4 to 10. Sunflowers love heat, and thrive in areas with long, hot summers (especially the tall, large-flowered varieties). Rudbeckias are short-lived perennials (meaning they die out after three or four years), but are sometimes treated as annuals in colder zones, such as 3 and 4.

SOIL Well-drained soil that is slightly acidic to somewhat alkaline (pH 6.0 to 7.5) and enriched with organic compost is best for sunflowers and rudbeckias. Sunflower roots need lots of space, so make sure that the soil is well dug and loose (but not so loose that the plants could blow over in the wind).

LIGHT As their name implies, sunflowers need sun—they'll bloom best when they receive eight to even twelve hours a day. Until the flowers mature, they will track the sun as it makes its daily voyage from east to west (a process called heliotropism). Rudbeckias are also best grown in full sun, especially the larger-flowered varieties; some smaller cultivars can grow in partial shade.

CHOOSING It is easiest to grow both rudbeckias and sunflowers from seed; choose seeds over potted plants if possible. Keep their different growing habits in mind; if you're looking to keep plants in your garden under 3 feet, you'll want to choose shorter rudbeckias over sunflowers.

PLANTING Sunflower and the smaller rudbeckia seeds germinate very quickly. The easiest method of planting is to sow seeds (¼ to 1 inch deep) directly in the soil after the last spring frost (once the temperature of the soil has reached 55 to 60 degrees). Perennials can be started in a cold frame in spring and moved when the plants have their first two to four true leaves. In general,

In the cutting garden at Skylands we grow dozens of varieties of sunflower and rudbeckia. 'Indian Summer' rudbeckias, bottom left, grow well in Katonah, as do 'Cherokee Sunset', 'Chim Chiminee', 'Goldilocks', and *R. triloba.* At right, a "volunteer," or self-seeding, sunflower turns its face to the sun on the east side of the cutting garden.

rudbeckias can be started inside but sunflowers grow best when they're planted directly in the garden and not transplanted.

Plant clusters of seeds 6 inches apart. (Not all the seeds will germinate; thin the hardier seedlings when they're about 6 inches tall.) If you're planting larger-variety sunflowers in rows, space them 30 inches apart. Rudbeckias self-seed heavily and spread easily, so you'll have many more plants by the second season. Space them about 18 inches or up to 2 feet apart.

WATERING Although sunflowers and rudbeckias are fairly hardy, they grow very rapidly and should be well watered about once a week, especially if you're in a dry climate (like the Southwest) or your region is experiencing a drought. If it's an exceptionally rainy season, you'll only have to water if the plants are germinating. Beware of overwatering, which can cause the roots to rot.

PRUNING Rudbeckias and sunflowers will bloom even more profusely when regularly deadheaded, so use your pruners to discard only spent flower heads. (I attach some of the cut, dried sunflower heads to the garden fences for the birds to eat. Butterflies love the seeds, too, which is a bonus if you want to attract them to your garden.) To save sunflower seeds for next year, cut the blooms off early (leaving about a foot of stem) and then hang them to dry in a dark, warm place away from hungry birds. Or, in the fall, once the back of the sunflower head has changed color from green to yellow, cut it off the stem and remove the seeds with your hands.

Saving rudbeckia seeds is even easier. Wait until the petals have all fallen off the blooms and the seedpods have turned light brown. Put a seedpod in a paper bag, and leave for a few days or up to a week to fully dry. Then spread the contents on a tray and separate the seeds from other material. Store the seeds in an envelope or a glass jar. Or use my preferred method and simply let the plant spread its seeds naturally—it can do all the work on its own.

TROUBLESHOOTING Some of the very tall or heavy-headed sunflower varieties may require extra staking during stormy weather. Although sunflowers and rudbeckias are generally quite robust and low-maintenance, powdery mildew, whitefly, and fungal leaf spots can present problems, especially in more humid climates. Use an organic fungicide and ensure the plants don't get too much water. A word of caution: Natural chemicals found in the hulls of sunflower seeds can be toxic to grasses (they're harmless to animals and humans). It's best to avoid growing sunflowers around grass you want to remain healthy.

HOW TO ARRANGE

CUTTING Like most flowers, sunflowers and rudbeckias should be cut either in the early morning or in the evening so they won't wilt quickly, as they would if cut at midday. It's best to cut when the petals are just beginning to unfurl (or at the bud stage; try mixing buds and blooms in arrangements). Cut stems at a 45-degree angle. For sunflowers, leave an average of 24 inches of stem (depending on the variety) on the flower head. Place the cut flowers in a bucket of water that is lukewarm to hot to soften the stems. Kevin also likes to cut sunflowers when they're past their prime and losing some petals. He removes the remaining petals and uses the dark flower center with its bit of green around the edges to add impact to an arrangement. Once cut, most varieties should last from a week to 10 days. Change the water daily to prolong the life of the blooms.

ARRANGING For a traditional tall sunflower, use an equally tall, bucket-shaped vase that's fairly substantial. An opaque vessel will hide the ungainly stems. If buds are going to be the focus of the arrangement, a lower vessel works better, to allow the buds' shape and texture to be seen and fully appreciated. To manage the branchy stems, insert them into a large flower frog or cage within a larger vessel. Sunflowers are terrific massed in a bunch or in a mixed arrangement of big-bloomed varieties such as 'Lemon Queen' and 'Mammoth', a fluffy 'Teddy Bear', and a dramatic red 'Infrared'. Kevin likes to pair sunflowers and rudbeckias with grasses or with other seasonal flowers, such as snapdragons, keeping the sunflower as the dramatic centerpiece. The leaves (on small-leaf varieties) are also beautiful, so look for foliage in good condition.

In a large ceramic mixing bowl, Kevin arranged a few armfuls' worth of rudbeckias, cut at varying heights for effect, and held in place with a cage frog. Varieties include 'Indian Summer', 'Prairie Sun', 'Cherokee Sunset', and 'Chim Chiminee', as well as *Echinacea purpurea*, which is another closely related member of the Asteraceae family. Some varieties of Echinacea are so similar to rudbeckia that they are both referred to by the common name of coneflower. Here, concentrating the purple coneflowers at certain focal points around the perimeter lends some order to the beautiful riot of blooms.

While many sunflowers have vibrant color, others, such as 'Strawberry Blonde', with their pale-yellow petals streaked with reddish brown, are more muted. Build upon the sturdy foundation of large flowers by adding visually lighter elements— feathery grasses, Queen Anne's lace—and selectively keeping some of the leaves. The natural texture of a vintage Asian coiled-wicker basket (it originally served as a teapot carrier) adds to the meadow effect. *OPPOSITE*: Play to your surroundings when thinking about arrangements. Here, a stunning collection of mixed sunflowers from the Skylands garden complements neutral walls and *faux-bois* furnishings. The rustic chair and birch bark container are reflected in the choice of the vintage Albany slip-glaze pitcher, which itself resembles wood. "It's hard to imagine this container holding anything but sunflowers," Kevin says. A few leaves are left on the stem to provide welcome touches of bright green.

A wicker French flower basket holds a collection of classic yellow sunflowers along with a mix of 'Indian Summer', 'Prairie Sun', 'Cherokee Sunset', and 'Chim Chiminee' rudbeckias, plus 'Oxeye sunflower'. Kevin took a multi-step approach to the unconventional vessel: first he lined the bottom of the basket with a tray, then added a wide bowl, using a tape grid (see page 262) for precise placement of each flower. *OPPOSITE*: Sunflowers are beautiful at all stages of their development and bloom. This arrangement will change dramatically as the large, tightly closed florets open day by day. At this stage, the accent is on the sculptural sunflower leaves and tight buds, combining the dark greens with the emerging warm yellows. You can enlist unexpected vessels, such as this antique pewter tureen, to hold arrangements. Chicken wire placed within the tureen holds the substantial flowers in place.

Dahlia

DAHLIA

ON ELM PLACE IN NUTLEY, NEW JERSEY, WHERE I GREW UP, THERE WAS A HOUSE AT THE BOTTOM OF THE STREET, RIGHT NEXT TO A LITTLE BROOK. I REMEMBER IT DISTINCTLY BECAUSE EACH SUMMER AND AUTUMN, THE SIDE YARD WAS FILLED WITH THE MOST AMAZING FLOWERS. THE GARDEN WAS SURROUNDED BY A WHITE PICKET FENCE; ON THE OTHER SIDE OF THE NARROW GATE GREW THE INCREDIBLE, COLORFUL BLOOMS MY FATHER TOLD ME WERE DAHLIAS.

The couple who lived there were proud of their dahlias. They knew each by name, and sometimes, if I asked nicely, they would let me into the garden to gaze with awe at the "dinner plates," the "pom poms," the "miniatures," and the "cactus." It was a riot of color, the plants staked upright to keep the blooms from sagging to the ground, and the garden was neat as a pin. I vowed to have a dahlia garden, sometime, somewhere.

That garden did not happen at Turkey Hill, in Westport, Connecticut, but I was inspired there, too, by two local gardens. One was on Maple Avenue, where a friend, an unlikely gardener, grew magnificent dahlias of all types in her side yard. That garden,

"DAHLIAS FILL AN IMPORTANT NEED IN ANY GARDEN. THEY ARE PRODUCTIVE AND USEFUL FROM LATE SUMMER UNTIL LATE FALL, WHEN MOST GARDEN FLOWERS HAVE ALREADY FADED."

also very neat and orderly, was regimented with 2-inch-by-2-inch stakes lined up geometrically, and tied with a spider net of twine to keep the dahlias straight as soldiers. And then I went to view the dahlias of the potter and artist Frances Palmer in nearby Weston, who had transformed an unused tennis court into her dahlia garden. Those exuberant flowers inspired her pottery with their distinctive shapes and textures, and again I vowed to create a dahlia garden of my own.

Finally, I did, and in the most wonderful locale: the cutting garden of Skylands in Maine. There, behind a lattice garden fence, 10 feet tall, protected from the rampant deer and porcupines, I planted my dream dahlias—the creams, the apricots, the pale pinks, the lavenders, the striped, and the splashed—from tiny to huge in size. And I realized why I had waited so long. Dahlias are so much better in a place of their own, in a garden where stakes and ties and narrow paths for grooming and cutting are permissible. These things are necessary to grow dahlias successfully, yet not very acceptable in formal borders or viewing gardens.

I have had the chance to get to know many of the country's best dahlia growers and learned much about how they care for and nurture their plants. I am still smitten with the giant 10- to 12-inch varieties, but I also like the easier-to-arrange smaller types, which come in such unusual sizes and formations. There are so many kinds that oftentimes it is difficult to comprehend that they are all dahlias! In arrangements, I prefer a profusion of all dahlias, of many types and colors. Kevin, on the other hand, will show off just two or three specimens, floating them in a shallow bowl, or more in a bouquet of mixed blooms and greenery. In any event, dahlias, like sunflowers and rudbeckias, fill an important need in any gardener's garden. They are productive and useful from late summer until late fall, when most other garden flowers have already faded and disappeared from the landscape.

Use coordinated dahlia blossoms or one large dinner-plate variety to construct a floating arrangement that is as much about the vessel display as it is the flowers. Working with a palette of pink for a dinner at Skylands (which included a pink granite dining table, pink Venetian glasses, and pink linen napkins), the pink and pinkish-yellow 'Jane Cowl' dahlias picked up on the undertones of the twentieth-century Indian brass bowl and serving tray.

DAHLIA **239**

GROWING
& ARRANGING

THE GENUS DAHLIA, *NAMED FOR EIGHTEENTH-CENTURY SWEDISH BOTANIST ANDREAS DAHL, OFFERS A VAST VARIETY OF BLOOMS— FROM FLOWER HEADS THE SIZE OF DINNER PLATES TO TINY TIGHT-PETALED POMS. THEY APPEAR IN COLORS FROM PALEST PINKS TO DEEP BURGUNDY BLACKS. SUCH VERSATILITY INSPIRES ALL KINDS OF CREATIVE POSSIBILITIES, IN THE GARDEN AND IN THE VASE.*

HOW TO GROW

Dahlias are easy to grow in most parts of the United States, but proper spring planting and winter storage are essential for success. Colors include white, pale to bright yellows, orange, bronze, pinks and purples, and all shades of red from fire engine to velvety maroon. Many gardeners also love their striking bicolors and variegates, such as 'Union Jack' and 'Deuil du Roi Albert', or those that boast colorful foliage, such as 'Bishop of Llandaff', a hot red-orange variety with purple-bronze foliage.

ZONE Dahlias are hardy in Zones 8 to 10, and can survive winters in Zone 7 with a thick layer of protective mulch. In these warm climates, dahlias can act as perennials, though some gardeners still dig them up each fall in order to ensure their vitality. My farm at Katonah is on the border of Zones 5 and 6, depending on the year, and Skylands (in Maine) is even colder; in areas like these, dahlias should be treated like annuals. We dig them up and store them with the first frost, then replant each spring (see Storage, page 245).

SOIL Dahlias need well-drained soil that's rich in organic matter, in an area that's sheltered from strong winds. Dahlias prefer a soil pH of 6.5 to 7.0, and the soil needs to be at least 60 degrees before planting, which is usually in late May or early June, depending on the region. In my gardens, we primarily amend the soil with farm-made compost, and add a dry, balanced fertilizer.

LIGHT Choose a location that gets a good amount of direct sunlight. My dahlias, like any in the Northeast, need full sun; dahlias in Southern regions can handle afternoon shade as long as they get at least six to eight hours of sunshine daily.

CHOOSING Dahlias for planting arrive in tuber form, a plant organ system that comes in all shapes and sizes depending on the variety. Tubers should be firm and dry, with no soft spots or disease. Once planted, the tuber will grow roots, which produce additional tubers (which can later be divided and replanted; see page 242), and the flower will sprout from the eye, or growth point.

PLANTING You can get a head start by potting the tubers indoors about a month before it's time to plant. Or you can skip this step and head outside once the soil is warm enough (at least 60 degrees). To plant, dig a hole 4 to 6 inches deep, set the eye of the tuber so it sits about 2 inches below the surface of the soil (whether in a pot or in the ground), then fill in with more soil and press down to remove any air pockets. Water the potted shoots thoroughly and place them on a warm, sunny windowsill until the weather

In the garden at Skylands, we grow many different single- and double-flowering varieties. Here a ball-shaped pom-pom dahlia, 'Ferncliff David Digweed', grows up to about 4 feet tall in the garden beds. The dahlias' usefulness as a flowering bush includes its ability to conceal large holes in a garden, especially in the late summer and fall when the rest of the garden may be past its prime.

is warm enough to transplant them outdoors. If planting larger varieties, such as 'Jane Cowl', be sure to drive stakes into the ground, 18 to 36 inches apart, ahead of planting in order to support the plants as they grow (see Staking, below). A full-size dahlia plant can easily fill a spot several feet across, so plan accordingly and make sure your dahlias will have sufficient room for air to circulate around them.

If you're in a warmer zone and your ground doesn't freeze as deep as the tubers are planted, they can stay put year-round. You may want to dig them up every couple of years, however, to check whether they need dividing. When a clump of tubers has appeared where one used to be, it's time to take pruners or a sharp knife and do some separating. Keep the neck of the tuber intact, and, when divided, make sure each piece has an eye. A single tuber can produce five to twenty additional tubers in a year of growth, making dahlia plants an excellent investment.

WATERING Tubers store the root systems, so do not water them too much at once before shoots emerge, to avoid possible rot. Understand the look and feel of your soil to judge whether the plant needs additional moisture; if hard-packed or slow-draining, water more gradually. Do not water until growth appears above the ground, when plants are 6 to 12 inches tall. Once plants are established, a deep watering twice a week will get them through summer dry periods.

FERTILIZING A week or two before planting, mix well-rotted manure, compost, or 5:10:10 fertilizer into the soil. At Skylands, the dahlias receive liquid fertilizer through the irrigation system every month. If you have a drip system or hoses set up, consider incorporating periodic fertilization. If you're more concerned with foliage than flowers, use a high-nitrogen fertilizer, which will promote foliage but reduce flower yield.

STAKING Most large dahlias need support via staking, as the flower heads can become too heavy for the stems. Before planting (to avoid injuring tubers), drive a heavy stake at least a foot into the ground, then plant tubers about 3 inches from the stake. As the dahlia grows, tie off every foot or so. At Skylands, we pound gray 1 by 1 wood stakes in between the plants,

Dahlias grow tall and proud, and to keep them that way, it's a good idea to support them with stakes. You can use bamboo or wood, as long as it's sturdy. In the dahlia beds at Skylands, a combination of cages, stakes, and a "cat's cradle" of twine allows the flowers to grow without drooping.

2½ to 3 feet apart, with jute twine spider-webbed down the row to help support the branches and blooms as needed.

PRUNING Deadheading is the key to keeping dahlias blooming. When your plant is 6 to 8 inches high, remove all but the strongest couple of stems. Prune deeply so that the plants do not become top-heavy and prone to breakage. To channel the plant's energy and encourage maximum bloom size (a must for show-quality entries), pinch off all of the smaller buds as they grow. To encourage a few big blooms at Skylands, we pinch the smaller buds lightly but not religiously.

STORAGE In colder climates and when treating dahlias as annuals, proper storage of the tubers between seasons is crucial. After the first frost, cut stems about a foot above the ground and carefully dig around the tuber clumps. Stay about a foot away from the stem when digging, to avoid bruising or spearing the tubers. Work slowly and gently knock off excess soil from the clumps. Then cut stems to a few inches, wash off the soil, and leave the tubers to dry, stems down. Set them in an airy place (not in the sun) to dry, until the soil easily shakes off. We dry our tubers indoors on racks for a few weeks, shaking off excess dirt and checking for rot and disease. Then we place them loosely in burlap sacks and store them in a dry attic or basement corner for the remainder of winter. You can also place the tubers in shallow cardboard boxes, covered with slightly damp sawdust, vermiculite, or a mixture of dry soil, peat, and sand, so only the stem pokes out. Some experts trim off the fine roots, too, and dip tubers in antifungal powder (such as lime and sulfur dust) before storing. The ideal storage temperature is 40 degrees, although anything between 34 and 50 degrees is acceptable.

Check the tubers' health every few weeks through the winter, and quickly discard any that look moldy or soft. Tubers that look shriveled should be misted with water until the sawdust is barely damp. If any tubers are slow to recover, remove them from the box for a few days and mist with warm water a couple of times. Even the most experienced gardeners lose a percentage of their tubers each year, so don't let it discourage you.

TROUBLESHOOTING Dahlias shorter than 8 inches are vulnerable to slugs and snails; pick them off if they appear. Control heavy aphid, earwig, or spider mite infestations with insecticidal soap. If dahlias show breakage and wilting, borers may be present. Deter them by keeping away weeds and cutting off any larvae-infested stems. Borers are an internal parasite, so spraying won't always remedy the situation. If they get too aggressive, simply remove the branches entirely. If you have leaf-hoppers, which feed on sap, spray plants with one tablespoon isopropyl alcohol mixed in one pint of insecticidal soap. Spider mites are especially tricky during hot, dry weather; spray undersides with neem oil or a jet of cold water. If powdery mildew appears (a whitish coating on the leaves), spray with wettable sulfur or another fungicide, and give plants more space for air circulation. Mildew, fungus, aphids, and whitefly are more likely in warm, damp weather. In Katonah and at Skylands, our dahlias are fairly disease free, but we spray them appropriately as needed.

HOW TO ARRANGE

CUTTING Flowers that are cut in full bloom tend to last the longest, but buds work well in arrangements, too. In general, select blossoms that are not too closed or too open. Make sure the petals don't come off easily, and strip the leaves from the stems. Use a sharp knife and place the cut stems directly into water. Dahlias can continue to bloom after cutting, so be judicious about where you're snipping on the plant. Kevin advises taking an occasional risk when cutting dahlias—consider a stem with a big flower and two buds; those buds may still bloom in the vase, or they may not, and that's part of the fun of including them.

MAINTAINING To get the most out of your cut flowers in a cool climate, place them in very hot water in the vase and let it cool. Warm water transfers up the stem faster, and is especially important with dinner-plate dahlias to ensure the big blooms don't become thirsty when freshly cut. Keep the cut flowers in fresh, clean water, changing it regularly to ward off bacteria. If the petals brown, simply remove and discard them. Dahlias can be long-lived because they are late-summer blooms—they're hardy enough to withstand a few cold nights.

ARRANGING Because dahlias come in all sizes, a variety of containers work well, from bud vases to punch bowls. A flower can stand alone as a single bloom, or settle nicely in a ginger jar with a mixture of sizes and forms. Like lilacs, they yield many flowers per plant, allowing for voluminous arrangements even from a small garden.

Dahlias can make beautiful foundations for seasonal fall bouquets, provide bright pops of color against darker-shaded autumnal foliage, or set a moody tone with their deeper, burnt hues. Try a mix of cultivars, such as round 'Paul Smith', scarlet 'Arabian Night', or flame-colored 'Fire Magic'. Beginning in late summer, dahlias pair nicely with plentiful chrysanthemums, chocolate cosmos, red and yellow zinnias, and sunflowers. Add texture with bright-red viburnum or *Skimmia* berries in a bouquet of copper-colored 'Autumn Joy' and russet dahlias, or surround bronze 'Pamela' dahlias with burgundy astilbe, velvety roses, and a border of red berries.

Dahlias are very exuberant flowers, so it is better to get playful with your arrangements than to try to control their shape in a static bundle. Use one color as a base, playing with another on top. A tape grid (see page 262) can work wonders with large, top-heavy dahlia blooms, helping to create volume, lend balance, or keep the flowers stationary in a shallow vase. You can also cut the stems on a slant, about an inch below the bloom, and float in tepid water. Try setting a flower upon the rim of a teacup; leave an inch of stem attached so the flower can drink.

The grand scale of dahlias invites you to arrange them in vessels that are larger and heavier than those you'd use with more delicate flowers. Take this tall, hefty Old French glazed earthenware crock that holds an oversize gathering of big late-summer 'Prince Noir' and 'Ferncliff Ebony' blooms, along with shoots of awakening buds. "The buds act as sparks," Kevin says, "so you don't drown in the mass of all these flowers." It's just right for the 14-foot-long kitchen table at Lily Pond in East Hampton.

A nineteenth-century tole tea tray holds all of the elements of an arrangement. The stems have been sorted and trimmed and extraneous leaves removed. This allows for a clearer focus on the composition from the outset.

OPPOSITE: Kiwi leaves and unripened berries from the garden at Skylands add a sweeping gesture and a dose of green to this dome of color-saturated blood-red 'Juanita' (a South African variety) and bicolor 'Kaiser Wilhelm' dahlias. The visual pop of brightness helps the eye appreciate and take in the deeply hued blossoms. An ornate Edwardian mirrored silver plateau further elevates the pressed-glass footed compote, turning a grand vase into a grander centerpiece for the room.

A large Staffordshire soup tureen, fitted with a giant flower frog, holds a stunning arrangement of three unusual fall blooms: 'Princesse Louise de Suede' striped dahlias in orange and white, papery Chinese lanterns stripped of all leaves, and dill turned to yellow flower heads. Though it was originally intended for the dinner table in a different context, the tureen offers the wide mouth and sense of abundance required for this arrangement. "This is particularly good as a table centerpiece," Kevin says, "because the flowers are at eye level and offer a close-up view of the beautiful petal structure." *OPPOSITE*: A great way to highlight one gorgeous flower is to gather several of its blooms to form a peak in a wide-mouthed vessel such as this segmented, three-tiered brass bowl, set on a mirrored faux-bamboo platter. This deceptively simple arrangement combines striped and solid dahlia varieties in oranges and reds with an exclamation point of yellow-and-burgundy-striped petals at the center.

An early autumn arrangement combines late-season 'Snoho Doris' dahlias with 'Chantilly' snapdragons and *Gomphocarpus physocarpus*. In a stout faux bois cylinder, the bouquet evokes a woodland theme. To construct it, Kevin started with a base of dahlias, then added the tall, spiky *Gomphocarpus*. The vertical lines help expand the scale of the arrangement without adding too much density, for an end result that combines all the beautiful last gasps of the flowering season. *OPPOSITE*: Lit up by the golden glow of autumn sunlight, the rich shades of burnt orange and rosy yellow complement the 'Ferncliff Ben Huston' dahlias and 'Autumn Joy' sedum. Studded with large, leathery leaves and delicate irises, this green and russet-hued arrangement mixes textures to great effect, with silky petals and rounded edges situated comfortably alongside fizzy flower clusters and rough-edged foliage.

For this centerpiece, a single 'Jane Cowl' dahlia bloom was snipped and set in the Chinese brass and silver-handled bowl embellished with a dragon. The blossom is positioned to look like an extension of the dragon. When setting a flower in a floating arrangement, be sure to leave an inch or so of stem attached so the bloom can con-tinue to drink. "There's a level of sophistica-tion to dahlias," Kevin says. "They're so beguiling, they can do anything. It's a flower that is just as beau-tiful in bud form as in full bloom, and you can make a big impact with just one blossom." *OPPOSITE:* The inherent drama of dinner-plate dahlias (here 'Jane Cowl') allows for simple, deliberate arrange-ments. Each miniature cylinder, fused together within the clear glass vase, holds an indivi-dual stem, precisely trimmed to the appro-priate height. With the vase providing support, the flowers can remain upright and showy—ready to embrace their well-deserved spotlight.

Arranging Flowers

Vases and containers are essential elements in the art of flower arranging. I discovered this very early on, when I created arrangements for my mother using cut flowers from my father's garden. We had a rather sparse supply of containers and I encouraged my mother to invest in more variety, despite her tight—oftentimes nonexistent—budget for such luxuries. I do recall using Ball jars, drinking glasses, teapots, and pitchers, filling them with masses of colorful tulips, handfuls of lilies, or gatherings of muscari and lilies of the valley that grew in profusion in the Elm Place garden. I started my own collection of containers when I got married; I was given incredible silver compotes, vases, a tea set, and various crystal vases, many of which I still have and use for flowers. On my travels and at the myriad tag and garage sales I frequented, I added to my growing assortment.

There are no rules for building a vase collection, but I can suggest that you choose vessels of varying sizes. Different widths and heights and depths will enable you to arrange all sorts of flowering and leafy materials. I particularly love ginger-jar shapes—the narrow mouths and copious bodies hold tall or short flowers upright and provide space for plenty

Just as planting a variety of flowers widens your possibilities for beautiful bouquets, having an assortment of vessels in a range of sizes, shapes, styles, and colors keeps things really interesting. This collection of containers in lustrous shades of soft gold and yellow includes, from left to right, a brass cauldron, a Venetian amber glass bottle vase, a twentieth-century Italian faience mantel urn, an Old Paris porcelain tureen, a Majolica pineapple sugar bowl, a gold vermeil etched vase, a High French classical urn, a flip glass, and a Chinese ginger jar.

of water. Accordingly, I have collected many clear blown glass, pottery, and Paris porcelain ginger jars. Wide bowls of all shapes, sizes, and materials can be fitted with flower frogs or grids of tape so flowers can be arranged nicely in masses.

Because these vessels can take up lots of space, it is imperative to find sufficient storage allowing vases, containers, and bowls to be housed and retrieved easily. I am fortunate to have a real flower room in my house in Maine that includes a sink room, a vase closet, and a refrigerator room where cut flowers and arrangements can be kept cool until ready to display. In the garage in Katonah, I created a room that doubles as a second prep kitchen as well as a flower-arranging space. Nevertheless, I still bring most flowers to the kitchen, where I can trim and prep and arrange right on the sink in the servery.

In addition to vessels, there are many other supplies that Kevin and I use every time we arrange blooms. These supplies can be found at flower markets, in many crafts stores, and online—a complete description of essential arranging tools can be found on the following pages. I suggest also reading up on other florists' techniques and instructions. You'll soon be well versed in creating arrangements that are memorable and distinctly your own.

In the greenhouse at Katonah, hydrangeas, phlox, coneflowers, apple branches, and yarrow soak in collecting pails full of water, while Kevin prepares an arrangement that also includes white hydrangea and the more unusual addition of rose of Sharon (*Hibiscus syriacus*). With its beautiful vase-shaped blooms and contrasting centers, rose of Sharon is a member not of the rose family but the Malvaceae (mallow) family. The flowers are fairly short-lived when branches are cut, however, so an arrangement that includes them is fairly ephemeral.

CHICKEN WIRE

SECATEURS

FLORAL GUM

FLORAL
WIRE

JELLY JAR

FLORAL
SHEARS

TOOLS

FLORAL
TAPE

To arrange flowers, you don't need
a lot of supplies or even much storage
space. In fact, all the necessary
materials can fit easily into a tool-
box or a drawer. Many of them
(including twine, plastic wrap, and
rubber bands) may be found in your
kitchen cabinets; the rest are
available at garden and home centers,
hardware stores, and nurseries.

FLOWER
FROG

TWINE

WATER
CAPSULES

RUBBER BANDS

PLASTIC WRAP

STEM STRIPPER

FLORAL
FOAM

FLORIST KNIFE

TRIMMERS

Just as cultivating a garden requires diligence and care, keeping your tools in top shape means maintaining them properly. Wipe damp spots dry every time you put tools away, for example, and refresh edges each season with a sharpening stone.

FLORAL SHEARS Use these short, serrated blades to trim pliable stems (like those of tulips or dahlias). The handles are designed to be nonslip and comfortable to hold.

SECATEURS Mini pruners like these can clip woody stems and branches with ease; switch to household scissors to clip off excess leaves.

FLORIST KNIFE A jack-of-all-trades tool, it slices through tough stems. For safety's sake, place the blade at an angle to the stem, then pull the stem away from you, using the pad of your thumb to control the blade, as when peeling an apple.

STEM STRIPPER This gadget lets you remove thorns and excess leaves without harming the stem. Kevin prefers the claw-shaped variety to disk-style strippers.

BUNDLERS

Chances are, you'll be submerging the following items in water, so make sure they are made from materials that won't deteriorate.

TWINE Reach for this when you need to gather a bunch of blooms or tie stems to a stake. Corralling a bouquet also makes it easier to keep flowers in place when cleaning the vase. Biodegradable natural twine is a better choice than nylon or acrylic twines; look for raffia, sisal, or jute.

FLORAL WIRE This flexible green aluminum wire blends in with stems. It's great for adhering stakes, pinecones, berries, and other accents. The higher the gauge number, the finer the wire; stick with finer gauges to avoid bruising stems.

RUBBER BANDS These offer a simple solution for gathering bouquets. Any household bands will do, but seek out clear or green elastics that will blend in with the stems when arranging in a transparent vase.

STABILIZERS

You probably won't need all of the following tools for simple bouquets, but they are useful in order to position flowers precisely in elaborate displays.

FLORAL GUM Tacky gum stabilizes flower frogs and protects vases from scratches. Also called floral adhesive or floral putty, it's nontoxic and easy to peel off, so it won't taint your water quality or vase. Kevin prefers floral gum sold in a roll, like tape, as it's easier to tear off pieces of the desired size.

FLORAL TAPE Water-resistant floral tape comes in two versions: a transparent tape perfect for making invisible tape grids (see page 262), and a stretchy, self-adhesive tape for making wreaths, boutonnieres, or corsages. The tape comes in multiple widths; the narrowest is generally the most useful. Opt for the stretchy kind (often green or brown) to bind stems and for flower crafts.

JELLY JAR Invert a jar within a vessel to add tiers to arrangements. Or use jars to corral flowers in bigger or less practical vessels (such as baskets)—simply affix to the bottom of the vessel with floral gum.

FLOWER FROG Made of metal, glass, or ceramic, flower frogs come in multiple shapes, sizes, and materials (see page 263 for examples). They help position and arrange floral stems; secure them to the base of your vessel with floral gum.

FLORAL FOAM An anchor for flowers and stakes, the spongy foam also supplies water to stems (see page 262 for more).

CHICKEN WIRE This stainless-steel mesh (also known as floral netting) can be used to make a support system to hold stems in place (see page 262 for more).

WATER CAPSULES Use one of these vials to keep flowers hydrated, not just in transport but also in a bouquet, when a stem is too short to reach the water in your vessel.

PLASTIC WRAP Line nonwaterproof vessels with this kitchen-staple-turned-liner to prevent rust and damage.

SUPPORTS

Structural supports keep arrangements looking tidy and polished and are essential if you're using certain vessels, such as a shallow dish or a wide-mouthed vase, to keep the stems stationary. You can of course use flower frogs (see opposite), which come in many shapes, types, and materials to suit different arrangement needs. Many florists use floral foam; Kevin and I tend to rely on other methods, but if you choose foam, seek out an environmentally friendly brand. (Oasis Floral Foam Maxlife and plant-derived Floral Soil are good options.) Make sure to saturate it thoroughly with water (this process can take a couple of hours) before cutting and inserting into your vessel. If you don't have a flower frog or foam on hand, below are two do-it-yourself options that will work just as well.

BUILDING A TAPE GRID
One of the easiest tricks for floral arrangements is creating a grid of tape across the opening of the vessel. "A tape grid creates the illusion of volume," says Kevin. "It can make just a handful of flowers look like twenty or more stems." A tape grid is especially useful for floppy flowers that require structural support. To build, attach strips of clear floral tape in a grid across the opening of the vessel (see photo below; we used green tape to demonstrate), with about ½ inch of overhang. Your grid size may depend on the size of stems you're using, but a general rule is to space your strips about half an inch to 1 inch apart. To secure, run another length of clear tape around the entire outside rim, trapping the overhanging ends. To hide the outer edge of tape, tuck foliage or small flowers around the rim of the container.

MAKING A CHICKEN WIRE BALL
If you're using an opaque vessel, you can use chicken wire to create a sturdy cage-style flower frog. Use strong clippers to cut a section of wire netting from the roll, and ball it up to fit inside your vessel, trimming as necessary (if scratching is a concern, first line the vessel with plastic wrap or use a slightly smaller bucket or jar as a liner). You can manipulate it within the vase to suit your needs; it should provide a handy set of spaces in which to insert each of your stems.

Flower frogs hold stems upright or at an angle. The objects, important in Japanese flower arranging, weren't actually called frogs until they made their way across the Pacific: Americans thought they looked like the amphibian, and the name stuck. Pincushion frogs have beds of needles (best for skinny stems like those of poppies); others may be sets of hairpin loops or domed cages (better for thicker stems such as lilies). You can also find novelty shapes—including flowers and, of course, green frogs. Some of the frogs in my collection are from flower or garden shops; others were antiques shop or flea market finds. Still others were a happy discovery in the flower room at Skylands, which overflowed with flower-arranging supplies when I bought the house.

VESSELS

Anything used to display flowers should be at once practical and decorative, serving as a tool and an aesthetic element. The right vessel can inspire an arrangement, emphasize its shapes and colors, highlight a particular flower, or lend sparse blooms a feeling of abundance.

CYLINDERS

With a similar diameter top to bottom, the simple geometry of a cylinder accentuates and props up gracefully arching stems of flowers like azaleas and tulips. The cylinder's modest lines also showcase twisted branches and whimsical vines without competing with them. Tall, wide cylinders work particularly well for long-stemmed blooms, such as sunflowers. Bundles of flowers that may slouch in a trumpet vase, such as poppies, are likelier to spring to attention in a cylinder of the same volume.

1 Swirl glass vase, 1930s, from Akro Agate, once the largest manufacturer of marbles in the U.S.

2 White pillow vase by McCoy Pottery, based on a Chinese design

3 One of a pair of 1930s copper fluted vases

4 Tall matte vase from the American Arts & Crafts movement

5 Jasperware prunus (tree blossom design) mantel vase

6 English stoneware jar from the 1920s, originally used for marmalade or mustard

7 Japanese lacquerware vase, likely an example of *maki-e* gold inlay

8 Early 1900s Fulper Pottery vase with Elephant's Breath glaze

9 Post-war German porcelain vase with molded flower design, by A.K. Kaiser

10 Silver thumbprint bud vase, by Elsa Peretti for Tiffany & Co.

SPHERES

These containers boast an ample interior and slightly narrower neck, and include fish bowl–shaped vessels, classic rose bowls (designed to prop up heavy blooms), and bubble bowls, as well as those more elongated at the top and bottom, such as ginger jars. Stems have room to spread out inside of the vessel, while the narrower mouth keeps blooms from flopping to the sides. Cluster flowers, including hydrangeas and lilacs, look especially charming in sphere-shaped vessels.

1 American pressed-glass rose bowl with inlaid sunflower pattern

2 Midcentury Revereware copper rose bowl, made in Rome, New York

3 1930s European Art Deco glass ball vase

4 Nineteenth-century glass, originally used as a fish bowl

BOTTLES

The slender neck of a bottle vase brings out the elegance of slim-stemmed blooms like roses or lilies. Display a bottle alone, in a pair, or lined up as a set. You can buy bottle vases, or repurpose containers intended to hold other things. If you're using more than one vessel in a display, vary the styles or heights to give the arrangement a sense of playfulness. Large bottles play up the minimalist look of flowering branches, such as magnolias. Small ones are perfect for single poppies or sprigs of wildflowers.

5 English green glass bulb-forcing vase (also known as a hyacinth glass)

6 Early-twentieth-century Japanese bronze bud vase

7 Bohemian spirits flask or decanter from the nineteenth century, originally used to sell liquor

8 Modern (1960s) Swedish blown-glass vase

9 Edwardian-era silver-plated bud vase

10 Tall smoked blown-glass vase from the 1970s

11 Jadeite bud vase made by Jeannette Glass Co. in the 1950s

12 Cylinder bud vase based on an apothecary beaker

13 Victorian water lens vessel, originally designed to magnify the light of a candle

PAILS

Buckets and urn-like vases gradually widen from bottom to top, though not as dramatically as trumpets (opposite). Fill the generous opening with billowy blooms of peonies or trumpet-shaped daffodils. The unfussy shape also imparts a less formal quality to flower-shop stalwarts like roses and lilies. Frogs and cages fit easily into pail shapes, affording you plenty of room to arrange flowers as you see fit.

1 Contemporary American earthenware cream-colored planter

2 Nineteenth-century English copper luster-ware bucket with relief molding

3 Vintage (1930s) fluted shot glass

4 Contemporary gilt striped porcelain vase

5 Stoneware flower-pot in gray finish by Ben Wolff Pottery in Connecticut

6 European flip glass with engraved landscape design

7 Vintage (1930s) ribbed copper flower pot

8 Silver-plated, handled ice bucket from the 1920s

LOW BOWLS

This shape is more versatile than you might think. Equipped with a flower frog or ring, it makes a striking foundation for graceful, flowering branches, such as azaleas, or a group of flowers with tall, sturdy stems, like lilies. Cutting the stems and floating a bloom or two in the water also makes a lovely centerpiece; flowers such as dahlias and camellias work especially well in floating arrangements. Keep the water level in the bowl high enough so that the bloom can sit above the rim and be observed from the side as well as from overhead.

1 Depression-era glass bowl based on the Tudor style

2 Old Paris porcelain openwork basket-weave vessel with attached gold rim and handle

3 Vintage green Depression glass (or "satin glass") flower ring, used to float small flowers within a larger vessel

4 Antique Japanese rusted cast-iron brazier, originally filled with lighted coals and used for portable heat

5 Late-nineteenth-century Japanese bronze low bowl

TRUMPETS

The conical structure of a trumpet vase shows off a burst of flowers with tall, graceful stems, such as lilies, tulips, or sweet peas. Radiating upward and outward, the flowers visually lengthen the curvature of the vase's rim. Parfait glasses are a good example of the trumpet shape; they work wonderfully for small arrangements.

6 Sterling-silver bud vase from the 1920s

7 English tall blown-glass trumpet vase

8 French floral-painted, gold-handled urn dating from 1810 to 1820

9 Venetian golden amber blown glass vase from the 1920s

10 French painted cast-iron trumpet vase, likely used as a memorial vase by a gravesite

11 Early-twentieth-century British white ironstone vase

FLOWER-SPECIFIC VESSELS

Vases have been a means for creative expression for almost as long they've been used to contain things. As craftsmen imagined forms to best accommodate regional flowers, their utilitarian task turned into an art form. Japanese flower baskets (*hanakago*), for instance, possess a haunting sculptural quality, taking on organic shapes and textures determined by the type of bamboo used and by the specific weaver's style. The striking spouts on the tulipiere, created by Dutch ceramists in the seventeenth century, accommodate not only tulips but also other blooms. Each spout pools into a common water reservoir— simplifying arranging and maintenance. I'm an avid collector of distinctive, flower-specific vessels like these, which are simultaneously functional and decorative. Learning about the origins of these pieces—and then sharing their interesting stories with others—is half the fun of collecting them.

1 Early 1900s Japanese bamboo basket designed for Ikebana (the art of Japanese flower arranging connected to the principles of a love of nature)

2 Tiered ceramic centerpiece, traditionally used to hold small spring bulbs; this one is from Martha by Mail

3 Green earthenware, lead-glazed paintbrush holder, purchased on a trip to Morocco

4 Early-nineteenth-century English creamware tulipiere, one of a pair to display on a mantel

5 Vintage Royal Haeger double-leaf ceramic vase with an open top

OPPOSITE: Tulipieres are designed for tulip arrangements, but don't have to be limited as such—it's fun to use different flowers and foliage like these clematis and many varieties of rhizomatous begonia leaves. (I have long cultivated an extensive collection of begonias, and especially love their interesting and spectacular foliage.) This Delftware tulipiere, with individual corner spouts and a water reservoir in each tier, shares its country of origin, the Netherlands, with the tulips themselves. Launched in the sixteenth century, Delft tin-glazed pottery is marked by its distinct blue and white colors and patterns.

1   2   3   4   5   6

UNCONVEN-TIONAL VESSELS

Even if you don't collect vases, it's likely you have interesting arrangement options in your closets and cupboards. Once you learn about the common forms that categorize most vases, you'll find potential in everyday items (shot glasses become bud vases; a soup tureen looks just right for an armload of fresh-cut roses). An unconventional vessel can accentuate aspects of your bouquet that a typical vase can't. Gather tropical lilies in a colorful pitcher and the room suddenly feels warmer; small buds in egg cups seem picked precisely for the kitchen counter; and hydrangeas set in a fishbowl add a playful touch to any room. There is often no such thing as the perfect vessel—an arrangement comes together when you concentrate on its character and what you'd like it to convey, and then select a vessel that brings that idea to life. Remember not to overthink it—so much of the joy in flower arranging comes from trying something unexpected.

1 Gold vermeil (gold-plated sterling silver) pitcher, circa 1920s

2 Large-scale American glass leech bowl, used by doctors in the nineteenth-century practice of bloodletting

3 English ironstone gluggle fish jug

4 Egg cup in drab-ware, the distinctive olive-colored glazed earthenware line from Wedgwood, first produced in 1811 (this one was sold by Martha by Mail in the early twenty-first century)

5 Vintage copper pudding mold, used for making cakes, jellies, and other desserts

6 Midcentury hand-painted Italian pitcher with woodland motif

7 Late-nineteenth-century Chinese hand-painted porcelain sauceboat in the form of a crane

8 Nineteenth-century Old Paris banded and monogrammed porcelain teacup and saucer

9 Painted parrot pitcher

10 Chinese export porcelain fish vessel, from the nineteenth century

11 Early-twentieth-century Japanese tetsubin teapot, fabricated in iron with a cherry-blossom motif

12 Silver lidded pumpkin jar

13 Early-nineteenth-century English creamware lidded soup tureen

OPPOSITE: This parrot pitcher (a house-warming gift from Lee Radziwill when I bought my house on Lily Pond Lane in East Hampton) works surprisingly well as a flower vessel. Here, it allowed us to take advantage of the inherent whimsy it lent to the arrangement of giant lily blossoms with fun foliage. Together, the two give the impression of a robust bundle of tropical flora. Because the mouth of the pitcher is small, leaving less room for thick stems, Kevin used just the heads of the lilies in order to take advantage of their miniature, slender stems. From above, you might not even realize there's anything special about the container—but it reveals an arrangement that packs a punch.

TECHNIQUES

PREPPING

Think of a flower's stem as its lifeline. When you keep it nourished, clean, and hydrated from the moment it's snipped, you'll end up with blooms that stay fresh and lively for up to a week and possibly even longer. A crucial part of any lasting arrangement is the care that goes into the flower before it's placed in the vase—and yet this is something many people overlook or underestimate. Kevin prides himself on getting the most from his arrangement flowers; here are a few of his most useful strategies.

TIME IT RIGHT Cut flowers from the garden in the early morning, when stems are firm and well hydrated, or wait until dusk, when they're well nourished. Avoid cutting in bright sunlight or the heat of the day; flowers will lose water more rapidly then. Make sure to use a clean, sharp floral knife, garden clippers, or shears. (Dull instruments will tear up the parts of the plant's stem that enable water delivery—leaving the blooms chronically thirsty.) Cut at a sharp angle, leaving a bit of stem on the plant, so there's opportunity for new blooms to grow. For flowers with nodes (azaleas, for example), snipping just *above* a node maximizes the plant's ability to absorb more water.

Don't forget to bring along a bucket of water—you'll want to place fresh-cut stems directly into it. If left out of the water for too long, cut stems can seal up and struggle to stay hydrated. Kevin and I always bring multiple buckets of varying sizes and heights, to organize and separate small, crushable flowers from large, heavy blooms.

CUT AND CLEAN Once you're indoors, refill all the containers with fresh water and recut the stems at a 45-degree angle. This maximizes the surface area for absorbing water, and keeps the stems from sitting flat on the bottom of the vessel and getting plugged up; strip off any leaves, thorns, and petals that will lie below the display vessel's waterline. (Because the flowers will be sitting in the vessel, excess materials can promote the growth of bacteria and compromise the stem's ability to hydrate itself, as well as cloud the water and cause unpleasant odors.) Trim away any spent blossoms, so the flower can focus its energy on the healthy blooms.

Some stems need extra help to drink up more water. In general, after cutting woody stems (such as lilacs, dogwoods, or azaleas) at an angle, use a knife to crosshatch (i.e., etch out an X on) the bottoms, or fray them with a hammer. The cut ends of milky flower stems (such as poppies, hollyhocks, or poinsettias) tend to get clogged by sap, so they should be dipped in boiling water (for about 30 seconds) or seared with a flame once cut. This seals the stem and keeps the flowers from losing nutrients.

CONDITION This step serves to fortify the stems, strengthening and stiffening them, so they hold up once they are arranged. Submerge the stems in any clean tall container, filled almost to the top with cool water. Place the container in the garage, basement, or another cool (not cold) area, away from direct sunlight, and let the stems soak up the water for a few hours, or even overnight. Some flowers, like daffodils and hyacinths, need to be conditioned in separate containers. They don't mix well with others, because the substance that makes them a natural pest repellent, calcium oxalate, is also toxic to other blooms. An overnight soaking will help them to release the calcium oxalate; once conditioned and well rinsed, they'll be ready to place in an arrangement.

DISINFECT While you're waiting, get your container ready. Make sure it's completely clear of any bacteria. Scrub the inside with mild dishwashing liquid and warm water or baking soda sprinkled onto a damp sponge; rinse well with warm water.

During dahlia season in Maine, the flower room at Skylands is lined with buckets of 'Ferncliff David Digweed', 'Prince Noir', and 'Brookside Snowball', among many others. All are gathered at their peak.

SHAPING

Flower arrangements generally fall into one of six basic styles. Envision what you'd like the general shape of your arrangement to be, pick the category (or two) that best describes it, and let the following steps guide you. And keep in mind that while a bouquet of wiry poppies might naturally fit into a wild, free-form display, don't be afraid to try something new and mass them together in a simple, structured dome.

DOME This classic curved shape works best with rounded blooms, like roses and peonies, and is best placed in areas where it can be viewed from all sides. To create the look, cut four or five stems so they're slightly longer than the length from the frog to the rim of the vase (spheres and bowls work best), and place around the rim. Repeat with four more flowers, cut slightly longer than the first batch, and insert them into the center. Fill in with flowers cut at varying lengths as desired. Rotate the bouquet and trim stems until you've created a rounded silhouette. Fill in bare spots with smaller blossoms or foliage.

SPIKY This silhouette is a natural choice for flowers with straight, sturdy stems and angular blooms (such as gladioli or delphiniums). If the mouth of the vase is wide (like this cylinder), make a tape grid to prevent leaning. For tall bouquets, start by arranging stems around the rim so they crisscross in the center and form a lattice just below the waterline; this acts as a second tier to support additional stems. Flowering branches and flowers that grow on stalks, such as azaleas and foxgloves, make excellent spiky, dramatic arrangements.

FREE-FORM Even the loosest style—with flowers allowed to bend and expand outside the borders of a traditional arrangement—requires some structural support. Begin with the tallest, stiffest branches, then add large, leafy stems to give you a canvas. You can nudge the geometry off-center to convey movement—these arrangements are great for alternative vessels. Next, add the biggest blooms and give your vessel a spin to make sure they are visible from every angle. Then add smaller blooms. Build on the natural twists and turns of the stems to give your bouquet personality. And it's important to remember: The arrangement includes the vessel. Blooms or foliage that spill over the vase can add to the overall impression.

GROUPED A solitary allium is striking, but gather a few into multiple small arrangements—each peeking from a container of a different height—and you have fireworks. Even when the result is more subdued, there's strength in numbers; a set of small, complementary bouquets adds up to a display with greater impact. Miniature vases on a footed platter can simulate a larger monolithic arrangement. Peonies, cut short and then placed in drinking glasses, make a pretty parade down the length of a table.

FLOATING A serene arrangement set drifting in a bowl is a simple way to save flowers with broken stems, but it's also a lovely intentional arrangement, especially for a dinner table. Cut stems to about an inch long and place in water. If the blooms sink, fashion a raft with a ring of bubble wrap slipped underneath. The best floating blooms have petals that spread out, including rhododendrons, daisies, dahlias, lilies, and garden roses.

SINGLE Simple and unfussy, an arrangement composed of a single, impressive flower in a bud or bottle vase invites you to observe details that might be overlooked in a bunch. Single arrangements require just the right kind of blossom, with a noteworthy size, color, or texture. A dinner-plate dahlia, a fluffy peony, a vibrant poppy, or an exuberant lily can captivate the viewer.

Dome

Spiky

Free-form

Grouped

Floating

Single

SCALE White peonies form the heart of this arrangement; Kevin chose the foxglove and grasses because of their ability to arc and bend, resulting in a composition with flowers about one and a half times the height of the vessel, his preferred ratio.

COLOR Existing entirely within a green and yellow palette, the accents of lady's mantle, foxglove, grasses, and variegated hosta complement the pale-hued peonies. Monochromatic arrangements have a seamless elegance; these color choices help to blur the lines between foliage and flowers.

TEXTURE The billowy, soft-petaled peonies in this bouquet are nestled within an atmosphere of competing textural elements: the airiness provided by the grasses offsets the densely packed flowers and foliage, and the structure of the large, rippled hosta leaf offers a tactile study in contrast.

COMPOSING

When an arrangement of flowers is just right, it simultaneously commands attention and fits in beautifully with its surroundings. Consider three important components as you start to consider your display: scale, color, and texture. Think of these guidelines not as rules, but as techniques that can help support any arrangement you create.

SCALE The scale of an arrangement refers to its size; a common ratio is about one to one, with the height of the flowers (from the rim of the vase to the top of the arrangement) about equal to the height of the vessel. Scale also refers to the arrangement as a whole—flowers, foliage, and vessel—in relation to its surroundings. To determine an appropriate scale for your arrangement, decide where it will sit in the room and whether there's a void to be filled vertically or horizontally (such as tall ceilings or an empty expanse of table). Consider the vantage point from which it will be viewed. A tall vase of long-stemmed sunflowers feels welcoming in the entryway, but would be awkward on a coffee table, where a few blooms floating in a shallow bowl (see the dahlias on page 238) invites conversation. If you're working with bunches of small flowers (see the sweet peas on page 132) or a single bloom cut short (like the poppies on page 161), use proportionate vessels; similarly, masses of flowers, like the lilacs Kevin arranged to make a grand statement at Skylands (pages 88–89), call for an equally enormous vessel. Once you've mastered the basic technique, experiment—Kevin prefers arrangements with flowers taller than the height of the vase; arrangements that break that rule, such as the peonies on page 113, can also be surprisingly effective.

COLOR Compositions work best when you keep things contained. If you're leaning toward a few hues, pick one to be the focus, and let the others serve as supporting players; unify the look by sticking with one kind of flower (see the daffodils on page 37). For a quick but graceful arrangement, group a single flower type by shade—a collection of pink, red, and orange zinnias (see page 127), for example—or arrange the color bundles alongside each other (see page 33). Choose colors that are adjacent to one another on the color wheel (red and orange tulips), or that offer a stark contrast (white and hot-pink peonies). Look to the plant itself for hints; pair orange and yellow blooms with foliage tinted with the same tones. The leaves will nestle in without clashing, and magnify the overall color effect. A specific container can provide inspiration, too, such as the yellow, peach, and mauve tree peonies in a Japanese jar depicting the same blooms (page 101).

TEXTURE An important consideration for the mood of the arrangement, texture provides dimension and substance, and introduces variety. Consider the texture of the flower petals and leaves, as well as the growing habit (overall shape) of a plant in the garden. Airy smoke bush, leathery rhododendron leaves, slender grasses, or delicate lady's mantle can transform an arrangement in different ways, softening or sharpening the overall impression. Gather similar textures to emphasize the effect (as in the spiky dahlias on page 249), or introduce something completely new, like peonies combined with swooping amaranthus (page 117). In a billowing cloud of hydrangeas (page 200), a sharp leaf adds contrast and allows the viewer to appreciate the different textural elements of the display. Consider the environment of the arrangement, as with the use of faux-bois vessels: see the rustic display of sunflowers on page 234 and the elegant roses on page 147.

Once you've decided on a plan for your arrangement, keep the look balanced by sticking with at least one unifying element, such as the flowers' color, size, or type. Spin the bouquet around as you work (use a lazy Susan, if you have one): examine it from all angles, both up close and at a distance, and make adjustments as you go. When you're adding finishing touches, remember subtle nuances. Kevin sometimes modifies individual blossoms, like inverting the petals of a showstopper tulip (see page 54) or turning over a leaf to reveal the underside (see page 220). Or switch things up to add visual punch—try a bright color, a "too-tall" vase, or a multitude of textures. You may end up with a dramatic, unexpected arrangement, and make some new discoveries in the process.

A CUTTING GARDEN

A cutting garden may seem like a luxury, but it's one that is accessible to anyone with a bit of land—even the corner of a yard—and the willingness, time, and energy to maintain it.

Until I purchased my home in Maine, I had never had a specific "cutting garden." My gardens in Westport, East Hampton, and Katonah were large enough and so densely planted that cutting enough flowers for arrangements was never a problem. The beds could lose a dozen stems of this or that and no one would notice. In Maine, the house gardens that surround the large stone terrace are designed to bloom from June until September. Planted with just enough to satisfy the eye, there is nothing that can be cut without upsetting the overall balance and beauty. Thus, I designed a giant cutting garden. Each year we determine which annuals to plant, and, because I am an aficionado of perennials, which bulbs and cultivars to add to the ever-growing collection of flowering plants, trees, and shrubs.

What we have used in the arrangements in this book visually explains the variety and scope of the plant materials that I love to grow and to bring into my homes. In Katonah, I make a point of growing thousands of daffodils, tulips, and small flowering bulbs, in addition to hundreds of peonies. At Lily Pond in East Hampton, my garden started as a rose garden; after redesigning and transferring the roses to Katonah, I now concentrate more on a formal garden, which is beloved by my friends for its lush shrubs, lilies, hydrangeas, and Japanese maples. In Maine, we concentrate on lilacs and hydrangeas and smoke bush for the giant arrangements. We also plant many hundreds of lilies, which bloom in midsummer, and dahlias for the fall.

IN AUTUMN
To plan out a cutting garden properly, you should start about a year in advance, preferably in the autumn, though it could also be done in the spring—as early as possible. Be aware that not everything grows everywhere, so read up on your zone and climate to learn which plants will thrive in your garden. Once you're ready to begin, the first step is choosing the location: cutting flowers need full sun and very good soil to produce the blooms that are worthy of arranging.

• Find a sunny spot that is protected from deer, rabbits, and other garden pests. (Fence it off and don't forget to install a good gate.)

• Stake out a shape that is pleasing and complementary in the landscape.

• Depending on the size of the garden, design a plan with paths and beds, using gardens you have seen (or studied in books and magazines) as inspiration.

• Strip the sod, if needed, and dig the soil to a depth of 18 inches or so. Test for nutrients, pH, and minerals, and amend where necessary. Add as much rich compost as you can, along with minerals and organic fertilizers.

• Access to water is essential, and a sprinkler system is a very good investment. Good drainage is also extremely important.

• Plan for a mix of perennials, biennials, and annuals. Do your research to understand the needs of each species or cultivar.

• Group plants with similar sun and watering needs, and consider the heights of plants when they're mature—tall plants should be placed where they won't block light from reaching other plants.

• Accumulate bulb and seed catalogs, and order when they arrive; seed catalogs start arriving in early winter.

• If you are in a cold climate, any plants planted in the fall must be carefully mulched after the ground freezes.

At Skylands, where I was able to create my first dedicated cutting garden, I chose a site right next to a large vegetable garden on the lower portion of the property, adjacent to the stable and carriage house. Along with numerous perennials, many strong annuals are planted to supply flowers for the smaller arrangements we place throughout the house.

IN SPRING

As the growing season begins, note the names and dates of what you plant; this will enable you to track your garden's progress.

• In very early spring, start seeds indoors to give them a head start. As the plants grow, transplant them into 2- to 4-inch pots for easy planting later in the garden.

• Visit plant centers and garden sales to stock up on wonderful seedlings that will immediately transform your garden into a beautiful and productive area.

• Plant more varieties, not fewer; you will have a more interesting garden, and much more interesting flower arrangements.

• Throughout the season, keep up with watering and weeding. Deadhead religiously!

• Stake tall plants prior to them growing too tall—use bamboo stakes or fine branches from black birch or a similar tree.

IN LATE SUMMER

Come late summer and into early autumn, as you put the garden to bed, revisit your original plan: what's working, what's not? Revise accordingly every year.

• When moving plants from one location to another, wait until they have finished blooming, cut them down to 4 inches or so, then water and feed transplants.

• Do not forget to feed regularly with organic fertilizers to ensure healthy growth.

• Finally, mulch as the weather cools.

The first year of the garden may not resemble exactly what you have in mind, but little by little, the plants will grow, the new additions will fill in the bare spots, and your vases will be overflowing with beautiful flowers.

In Katonah, I grow flowers and foliage everywhere. The cutting garden, located between the main greenhouse and equipment barn, is no exception, and has been well planned. I wanted the plants to be varied, so every bed is mixed; some of the greatest delights in any cutting garden are the "volunteer" flowers that self-seed across and among the beds.

ACKNOWLEDGMENTS

Many people are to be thanked for their help with this book. Many have never visited my gardens, but they have provided me with many of the plants and seeds and bulbs and shrubs that fill those gardens. They have been instrumental, through their exquisite catalogs and with their superb plant materials, in making my gardens the interesting sources for most everything Kevin and I used in the photographs for this book.

I especially want to thank, in no particular order, the following plantsmen and women: Brent and Becky's, Van Engelen, B&D Lilies, Van Bourgondien Nursery, Johnny's Selected Seeds, Vilmorin, David Austin Roses, Marders, The Bayberry, Landcraft Environments, Broken Arrow Nursery, Glover Perennials, Hardscrabble Farms, Surry Gardens, Burpee, Home Depot, Proven Winners, Annie's Annuals & Perennials, Rainbow Iris Farm, Peony's Envy, Klehm's Song Sparrow Nursery, Opus, Hillside Nursery, and Old House Gardens.

And a great big thank you to my current gardeners who nurture the plants and tend to my gardens all year long: Ryan McCallister and Wilmer Artiga and the Katonah crew, Alex Silva and his East Hampton crew, and Michael Harding and his Seal Harbor crew. Thanks also to all the fine hands who have cared for all of my gardens in past years.

Kevin Sharkey and I would also like to extend our thanks to our editorial director, Ellen Morrissey; managing editor Susanne Ruppert; senior associate editor Bridget Fitzgerald; Nanette Maxim; the designer of this volume, Mary Jane Callister; and all the photographers and stylists who aided us while flowers were cut, backgrounds were styled, and arrangements created. Thank you as well to Maison Gerard for graciously loaning us the beautiful tulipiere by Matthew Solomon, pictured on page 8.

And thank you to my longtime publisher, Clarkson Potter, for allowing us to make such a lavish, beautiful, useful book—our ninetieth, give or take one or two!

PHOTOGRAPH CREDITS

SANG AN: page 166

CHRISTOPHER BAKER: pages 33, 50, 53

EARL CARTER: page 252

JOHN DOLAN: pages 28, 31, 36, 99, 133, 275 (top center)

PIETER ESTERSOHN: page 237

RICHARD FELBER: page 191

KRISTINE FOLEY: pages 97, 115, 118

FORMULA Z/S: page 198

DOUGLAS FRIEDMAN: pages 88–89

DANA GALLAGHER: page 185

BRYAN GARDNER: pages 219 (right), 221, 223

GENTL AND HYERS: pages 6, 113, 121, 123, 276

GABRIELA HERMAN: pages 14, 64, 67, 73–74, 77–79, 81–82, 86, 87, 90–91, 105 (top), 124, 180, 187–188, 193 (left), 194–195, 197, 203, 207, 210–211, 214, 271, 275 (top and bottom right)

LISA HUBBARD: pages 141, 170

STEPHEN KENT JOHNSON: page 19 (left)

ANDREA JONES: page 193 (right)

MIKE KRAUTTER: page 220

FREDERIC LAGRANGE: pages 49, 57, 59, 101, 114, 119–120, 142, 145, 147, 151, 213, 219 (left), 250

KATE MATHIS: pages 23–24

CHELSEA MCNAMARA: pages 16, 39, 43, 47–48, 51, 52, 55

DAVID MEREDITH: pages 27, 54, 127 (left), 128, 130–131, 153, 179, 233, 235, 275 (top left)

NGOC MINH NGO: pages 10, 85, 199, 209, 212, 215–216, 225, 229 (top), 232, 238, 241–245, 247–249, 251, 254, 273, 275 (bottom center), 279–281, 288

VICTORIA PEARSON: pages 200–201

JOSÉ PICAYO: pages 2–5, 9, 19 (right), 21–22, 40, 44, 58, 60–61, 63, 68–69, 71, 93–94, 98, 102, 105 (bottom), 106–109, 111, 116–117, 122, 127 (right), 129, 132, 135–136, 139, 146, 149–150, 152, 156–157, 159, 161, 163–165, 167, 169, 173–174, 176–177, 183, 192, 204, 226, 229 (bottom), 231, 234, 253, 257–258, 260, 262–269, 275 (bottom left), endpapers

ANNIE SCHLECHTER: pages 222, 255

MATTHEW SEPTIMUS: pages 32, 34, 37

SETH SMOOT: page 25

ANNA WILLIAMS: page 7

INDEX

in arrangements, *237–38, 247–55*
cutting and arranging, 246
in the garden, *241, 242–43*
growing tips, 240, 242, 245–46
daisies, *203*
    See also sunflowers and rudbeckias
delphiniums *(Delphinium)*, 178–85
    about, 178–81
    in arrangements, *179–80, 185*
    cutting and arranging, 184
    in the garden, *183*
    growing tips, 182, 184
Dianthus, 114, 133, 153, 180
Dicentra (bleeding heart), *49, 87*
Digitalis (foxgloves), *127, 133, 276*
dill, *250, 252*

E

Echinacea purpurea, 231
Elizabeth and Her German Garden (von
    Arnim), 72
Ely, Helena Rutherfurd, 178

F

Farrand, Beatrix, 65
ferns, 148, 162
    in arrangements, *49, 123, 150, 169, 215*
filbert leaves, *203*
foliage, 84
    autumn leaves, *219, 220, 223*
    See also ferns; *specific plants*
forget-me-nots, *87*
forsythia, 25
foxgloves, *127, 133, 276*
fritillaria
    in arrangements, *19, 50, 53, 54, 87, 153*
    crown imperial, 45, *50, 54*
    with tulips, 47
frogs, 261, 262, *263*
fruit-bearing branches, *203*, 218, *219*, 246, *249*
    See also specific types
fuchsias, 112, *118*

G

garden books, 11, 12, 72, 178
garden calendars, 18
garden planning
    a cutting garden, 278, 280
    inspiration sources, 11, 12
    Martha's gardens, 11–15
garlic chives, 95
geranium leaves, *54, 57, 147*, 148
gladioli, *131*
Gomphocarpus physocarpus, 219, 222, 253
grapevines, *225, 227*

grasses, in arrangements, *34, 120, 164, 233, 276*
Greenfield Hill garden (Connecticut), 13, 65
Gunnera, 163
Gurvich, Ruth, *123*
Gypsophila, 148

H

Helianthus. See sunflowers and rudbeckias
hellebores, *23, 90, 129, 147*
Heuchera leaves, *53, 101, 116, 118, 221*
Hibiscus syriacus, 258
Hinkley, Dan, 189
hollyhocks, *180*
horse chestnut, *22*, 84
hostas, *10*
    leaves in arrangements, *115, 119, 120, 129,
        276*
Hyacinthoides. See wood hyacinth
hydrangeas *(Hydrangea)*, 186–201
    about, 186–89
    in arrangements, *180, 187, 195, 197–201,
        219, 258*
    cutting and arranging, 196
    in the garden, *191–92*
    growing tips, 190, 194, 196
    species and varieties, 186, 189, 193

I

iris, 112
ivy, *50*

J

jasmine, *147, 153, 200*
Jensen, Jens, 13, 205

K

kale, ornamental, *223*
kiwi vines, *249*
Klehm, Roy, 100, 103
knotweed, Virginia, 162

L

lady's mantle *(Alchemilla)*, 41
    in autumn arrangements, *223*
    with columbine, *21*
    with daffodils, *32*
    with peonies, *119, 120, 276*
    with poppies, *163, 164, 167*
    with roses, *146*
Landcraft Environments, 205
Ligularia, 48
lilacs, 72–91
    about, 72–75
    in arrangements, *39, 53, 55, 61, 73, 85–91*
    companion flowers, 35, 47, 56, 84

MARTHA STEWART is America's most trusted lifestyle expert and teacher, and the author of more than 80 books on cooking, entertaining, crafts, homekeeping, gardening, weddings, and decorating.

KEVIN SHARKEY, Executive Director of Design at Martha Stewart Living, helped found the decorating and floral-design voice of *Martha Stewart Living* magazine, working alongside Martha for 22 years.